Mary Berry's MAIN COURSE

Cookery Adviser: Jane Grigson

Also by Mary Berry and published by Batsford:
Cooking with Cheese

Mary Berry's
MAIN COURSE

B T Batsford Ltd London

First published 1981

ISBN 0 7134 0920 7 Hardback
     0 7134 0921 5 Limp edition

Phototypeset in Linotron 202 Palatino by
Western Printing Services Ltd, Bristol
Printed in Great Britain by
The Anchor Press, Tiptree.
for the publishers, B T Batsford Ltd
4 Fitzhardinge Street, London W1H 0AH

Contents

Introduction

Lunch, dinner, supper . . . a lunch party for a few friends, a special occasion dinner with all the trimmings, family supper . . . they are all based on *something*. Whether you are serving a one-dish meal cooked and brought to table in a casserole with all the vegetables incorporated, or whether your dinner party menu involves a variety of preliminary courses, plus pudding or dessert, the simple truth is that the success of the whole thing rests on the main course.

It may be fish, it may be meat, poultry or game, it may be inexpensive mince, pasta or rice, or vegetables. It may be home-made pâté with brown bread and butter or it may be an elaborately cooked saddle of lamb. It may take hours of preparation or it may be on the table in minutes.

It is the main course and it deserves your attention. Above all, think before you cook; it is the way to avoid wasted time and money and prevent disappointment. Plan your menus round the main dish. If steak and kidney pie is to be the high spot of the meal, you won't serve apple tart afterwards, any more than you will serve a very rich sweet after roast duck.

Think too about what you will need. It goes without saying that you shop in advance for the important ingredients, the crown roast of lamb, for instance, that your butcher has to prepare for you. But to find, when you come to prepare the stuffing, that the dried apricots and the walnuts are missing and the shops are shut, is disaster.

Similarly, have all your ingredients to hand when you start cooking. Many of them – breadcrumbs for stuffing, vegetables to go with the meat – can be got ready well in advance. Have ready too all pans and cooking utensils that you will need – the electric mixer, the measuring jug, the colander for the vegetables. Just a little thought along these lines and the most ambitious dinner party loses its terrors.

Not only big occasions but everyday meals need planning. Variety is the spice of cookery and the family cook has every chance to practise it. Repetition is boring, so don't be afraid to experiment; husbands and children can be surprisingly adaptable to new dishes.

When you are deciding on the centrepiece of your menu, pick on something appropriate to the time of year, the ingredients at hand and the time available for preparation and cooking.

Cost comes into it too. Of course it does. If it is a celebration dinner party you will be prepared to splash out – on saddle of lamb perhaps, or fresh salmon. You will be prepared to spend time and take trouble in the kitchen, to make the perfect mayonnaise, to ensure that the vegetables are cooked to perfection. For more everyday occasions, balance the budget by using up all leftovers, minced beef, chopped bacon; fill out family dishes with pasta, rice, mashed potato. These can be very popular. Many children, for instance, prefer a good shepherd's pie to the best steak – I know that mine do.

Food in season costs less. Make tomato dishes in late summer when tomatoes are plentiful and cheap. Use vegetables from the garden or the market. Buy fresh fish when there is a glut and prices are lower – you can always freeze what you do not use if you have a freezer.

Long, slow cooking in a casserole makes the most of cheaper, tougher cuts of beef, and you can cook the vegetables along with it, saving fuel and making serving easy.

Ring the changes on the potatoes theme by serving buttered noodles, pasta shells or boiled rice.

Take trouble over shopping. Buy really fresh fish if you are lucky enough to have a good fishmonger and cook it as soon as you can. Make friends with your butcher and ask his advice about best buys. He may be able to provide specialities like veal and sweetbreads which are not always easy to come by.

Fresh vegetables and fruit are often good bargains in local markets and in summer you may be able to take the growers' offer to pick your own. Look at any bargain offers in your supermarket. Use your freezer to store what you do not need immediately.

So make up your mind. What are you going to spend? What time have you got? What short cuts can you take when time presses?

For meals in a hurry there is grilling and frying. Both methods are quick and a meal can be on the table in minutes. The addition of a well-flavoured sauce is probably all that is needed. For quick sauces use canned soups – mushroom, chicken, asparagus – or stock cubes, chicken or beef. These will go, too, into a quickly prepared casserole which can be left to cook slowly until it is required.

Sauces and stuffings are indeed a valuable part of any main dish. In them you can combine interesting flavours and achieve a contrast in textures. Use herbs and spices to give the dish a lift and add wine or cider to give extra flavour. For omelettes add cream for extra richness. For meat, for fish and for vegetables, the sauce makes the dish, and a good stuffing not only enhances meat and poultry – it makes them go further too.

Then there is appearance. A few minutes' thought on what goes with what pays dividends in stimulating appetites. For example, just take green vegetables with white fish – peas, sliced green beans, watercress, parsley in a white sauce – these make all the difference to what otherwise might be good but dull. For colour and variety there are garnishes of tomato, green or red peppers, golden sweet corn, black olives.

Let your cookery be imaginative. Choose dishes that are appropriate to the season of the year, using the best and freshest materials available.

Consider, too, the time you have for preparation and cooking and think of who is going to eat the end product.

Balance your menu. Make sure the rest of the meal does not fight with the main course. Serve the appropriate vegetables and sauces. Take trouble. Garnish and decorate dishes so that they are appetising to look at but not over-elaborate and fussy.

Party food, family meals, light lunches or suppers – they all have their special characters and their separate needs. There is something for all of them in the recipes that follow. Try them.

Acknowledgment

All these recipes have been well and truly tested and I am very grateful to Clare Blunt who has been meticulous with her recipe development work for this book, as always.

The Meat Promotion Executive provided the colour photographs of lamb kebabs, braised oxtail, navarin of lamb and braised beef in red wine.

FAMILY FISH DISHES

Who wouldn't want to come in from the cold to a hearty fish pie straight out of the oven, crisp and golden on top, bubbling with cheese sauce inside, creamy with mashed potato?

Fish is the family cook's friend. Children love it, it is a favourite with grown-ups, for lunch, dinner or supper, nourishing and easy to digest, appetising in flavour; served with potatoes or rice it is economical and satisfying.

Haddock, cod, lemon sole and plaice are the basis of many dishes. The simplest fish becomes inviting when dressed up and well flavoured. Cheese, hard-boiled eggs, tomatoes and mushrooms are all natural partners for white fish. Recipes can be adapted to use what is available and a good buy at the time. Smoked haddock or cod give distinctive flavour to kedgeree or fish soufflé. The oily fish, herrings and mackerel, are best grilled, fried or baked with the addition only of a piquant sauce.

When you shop for fish, buy the freshest you can find and cook white fish the same day – smoked will keep for several days in the fridge, well wrapped. If you cannot get really fresh fish, use frozen; keep a supply of it in the freezer. And of course you can freeze most kinds of fish and prepared fish dishes.

The recipes here are tried family favourites. Serve them with green vegetables for extra nourishment.

Somerset fish   *Serves 4*

A simple fish dish that looks very attractive. Use any white fish that is a good buy at the fishmongers.

550 g (1¼ lb) skinned white fish   *450 g (1 lb) cooked mashed potato*
8 button mushrooms   *25 g (1 oz) butter*
2 tomatoes, skinned and quartered   *25 g (1 oz) flour*
Salt and pepper   *25 g (1 oz) Cheddar cheese, grated*
300 ml (10 fl oz) dry cider

Cut the fish into neat cubes and place in a shallow pan with the mushrooms and tomatoes and season well. Pour the cider over and simmer gently for 15–20 minutes or until the fish is tender and will flake.

Meanwhile pipe or fork a border of mashed potato around the edge of a shallow ovenproof dish.

Lift out the fish, mushrooms and tomatoes with a slotted spoon and put in the potato border, keep the cider remaining in the pan.

Melt the butter in a small saucepan and add the flour and cook for a minute, blend in the cider and bring to the boil, stirring until the sauce has thickened. Taste and check seasoning and then spoon over the fish.

Sprinkle with the cheese and then brown under a hot grill. Serve with a green vegetable such as peas or runner beans.

Haddock wylie   *Serves 4*

A tasty fish dish that may be prepared in advance and reheated when required.

450 g (1 lb) haddock
300 ml (10 fl oz) milk
2 hard-boiled eggs, sliced
25 g (1 oz) butter
25 g (1 oz) flour
Salt and pepper

1 tbsp lemon juice
1 tbsp chopped fresh parsley
3 tbsp oil
50 g (2 oz) fresh white breadcrumbs
2 tomatoes

Put the fish into a pan with the milk and lightly poach for 10 minutes or until the fish can be easily flaked with a fork. Strain the milk from the fish, then skin and flake the fish, removing any bones and place in a buttered ovenproof dish, cover with slices of hard-boiled egg.

Rinse out the pan, then melt the butter in it and stir in the flour, cook for 2 minutes. Blend in the milk and bring to the boil, stirring until thickened and simmer for 2 minutes. Season well and beat in the lemon juice and parsley and pour over the fish and eggs.

Heat the oil in a small frying pan and fry the breadcrumbs until they are a pale golden brown all over, stirring frequently; spoon over the fish.

Cut the tomatoes in slices and arrange around the edge of the dish.

Bake in a hot oven 200° C (400° F), gas mark 6 for about 20 minutes or until it is hot through. Serve with a green vegetable such as peas or green beans.

Malvern cod   *Serves 4*

A quick and simple supper dish for a working wife. Cook the rice the evening before and leave it covered in the fridge until the next day. At the same time put the cod steaks in the fridge to thaw. The next evening assemble the dish and bake and the meal will be on the table in under an hour. Serve with French or runner beans or, if prefered, a green salad.

175 g (6 oz) long grain rice
4 frozen cod steaks, thawed
25 g (1 oz) butter
25 g (1 oz) flour
300 ml (10 fl oz) milk
Pepper and salt
225 g (8 oz) tomatoes
100 g (4 oz) cheese, grated

Cook the rice in boiling salted water for about 12 minutes or until tender, rinse and drain thoroughly.

Well butter a large shallow ovenproof dish and place the rice around the edge of the dish. Put the cod steaks in the centre.

Melt the butter in a small pan, add the flour and cook for a minute. Add the milk and bring to the boil, stirring until thickened, simmer for 2–3 minutes and season well, then pour over the cod.

Thickly slice the tomatoes and arrange on top of the rice around the edge of the dish. Sprinkle the grated cheese all over the dish.

Bake for 30 minutes in the centre of the oven at 200° C (400° F), gas mark 6 until the cheese is golden brown and the fish tender.

Kedgeree   *Serves 4*

Some people put sultanas in a kedgeree but for my taste I prefer it without.

175 g (6 oz) long grain rice	*50 g (2 oz) butter*
Salt	*1 tbsp lemon juice*
2 hard-boiled eggs	*Cayenne pepper*
350 g (12 oz) smoked haddock fillet	*Sprigs of parsley to garnish*

Cook the rice in plenty of boiling salted water for 12 minutes or until the rice is tender; rinse well and drain and keep warm.

Roughly chop the eggs, but reserve a few perfect slices for garnish.

Poach the smoked haddock in a little water for about 10 minutes. Drain and remove all skin and bones and flake the fish.

Melt the butter in a large pan, add the rice, chopped eggs and fish and heat through slowly; stir in the lemon juice and salt and cayenne pepper to taste. Pile into a warm dish and serve garnished with parsley sprigs and slices of egg.

Baked mackerel with mustard sauce   *Serves 4*

Mackerel must be really fresh; look out for a shiny, slippery skin on the fish and bright eyes, and of course a nice fresh smell! If you are not fond of stuffing in fish just bake them covered with a buttered paper and serve with the sauce.

4 small mackerel, filleted, with the	*Grated rind of half a lemon*
* tails left on*	*1 tsp lemon juice*
50 g (2 oz) fresh white breadcrumbs	*½ tsp dried thyme*
1 stick celery, chopped	*Salt and pepper*
1 heaped tsp chopped parsley	*25 g (1 oz) butter*

Sauce

25 g (1 oz) butter	*About 1 tbsp made mustard*
25 g (1 oz) flour	*1 tbsp cider or malt vinegar*
300 ml (10 fl oz) milk	*2 tsp caster sugar*
Salt and pepper	

Slices of lemon to garnish

Heat the oven to 200° C (400° F), gas mark 6.

Wash the mackerel and dry thoroughly on kitchen paper. Put the breadcrumbs in a bowl with the celery, parsley, lemon rind and juice and seasoning.

Melt the butter and stir into the breadcrumbs to bind the mixture which should be moist and crumbly. Divide the stuffing between the fish and then press the fish back into shape. Slash the skin twice on each side.

Well butter a shallow ovenproof dish and lay the fish in it. Cover with a lightly buttered piece of greaseproof paper and bake for 25–30 minutes in the oven.

Meanwhile make the sauce: melt the butter in a small pan, stir in the flour and cook for a minute. Blend in the milk and bring to the boil, stirring until thickened, add the remaining ingredients to the sauce and simmer for 3 minutes.

Garnish the fish with slices of lemon and serve the sauce separately.

Baked cod with courgettes and tomatoes   *Serves 4*

If you haven't the oven on for something else you could grill the cod on both sides and then serve with the vegetables.

1 tbsp oil	*225 g (8 oz) tomatoes, peeled and*
1 onion, chopped	*quartered*
225 g (8 oz) courgettes, sliced	*Salt and pepper*
1 clove garlic, crushed	*4 cod steaks*
	Butter

Heat the oven to 180° C (350° F), gas mark 4.

Heat the oil in a pan, add the onion and fry gently without colouring for 5–6 minutes, then add the courgettes, garlic and tomatoes, season well and bring to the boil.

Lightly season the cod steaks on both sides and then lay in a single layer in a shallow ovenproof dish and pour the hot vegetables over. Dot with a little butter and bake in the oven for about 30 minutes or until the fish is cooked.

Soufflé fish pie   *Serves 4*

This is a good family supper dish, that may be made from ingredients in the cupboard.

40 g (1½ oz) butter
40 g (1½ oz) flour
450 ml (15 fl oz) milk
Salt and pepper
1 tbsp chopped parsley

200 g (7 oz) can tuna fish,
  drained and flaked
2 eggs, separated
50 g (2 oz) grated cheese
½ level tsp made mustard

Heat the oven to 200° C (400° F), gas mark 6. Well butter a 17·5 cm (7 in) square dish.

Melt the butter in a saucepan, add the flour and cook for a minute. Add the milk and bring to the boil, stirring until thickened, cook for 2 minutes and season well. Put half the sauce in a bowl and stir in the parsley and tuna fish, mix well and spread over the base of the dish.

Stir the egg yolks, grated cheese and mustard into the sauce remaining in the pan.

Whisk the egg whites until stiff using a rotary or electric hand whisk and fold into the sauce. Spoon on top of the tuna fish, spreading right up to the edge of the dish and bake in the oven for 30–35 minutes until the soufflé is well risen and golden brown.

Serve at once with chopped spinach or a green vegetable.

Baked haddock with mushroom sauce   *Serves 4*

If you have difficulty in getting fresh haddock use instead bream or any white fish fillet.

550 g (1¼ lb) skinned fresh haddock fillet

Sauce
25 g (1 oz) butter
1 onion, finely chopped
100 g (4 oz) mushrooms, sliced

25 g (1 oz) flour
300 ml (10 fl oz) milk
Salt and pepper

Topping
2 tbsp browned crumbs

2 tbsp melted butter

Heat the oven to 180° C (350° F), gas mark 4.

Cut fish into serving portions and lay in a single layer in a shallow ovenproof dish that has been lightly buttered.

Now make the sauce: melt the butter in a small pan, add the onion and cover and cook gently until soft but not brown, about 10 minutes, then add the mushrooms and cook gently for about 3 minutes, stir in the flour and cook for a minute. Blend in the milk and bring to the boil, stirring until the sauce has thickened, season well and pour over the fish.

Sprinkle with crumbs and then drip over the melted butter.

Bake in the oven for 20–25 minutes or until the fish is cooked and will flake. Serve with sauté potatoes and green peas or beans.

Prawn vol au vent   *Serves 3*

This is a very good way of serving prawns as it makes a small quantity go quite a long way.

397 g (14 oz) packet puff pastry, thawed	*1 tsp tomato purée*
Milk or beaten egg to glaze	*100–175 g (4–6 oz) peeled prawns*
25 g (1 oz) butter	*Salt and pepper*
25 g (1 oz) flour	*1 level tbsp chopped parsley*
300 ml (10 fl oz) milk	*2 tbsp sherry, optional*

Heat the oven to 220° C (425° F), gas mark 7.

First make the vol au vent cases.

Roll out the pastry to 0·60 cm (¼ in) thickness on a floured table. Cut into 4 circles with a 7·5 cm (3 in) cutter, then re-roll the trimming and cut out a further 2 circles, make a smaller cut inside each case but do not cut completely through. Place on a baking sheet and then chill in the refrigerator for 30 minutes. Brush the tops with beaten egg or milk and bake for about 20 minutes or until well risen and golden brown. Remove from the oven and lift onto a wire rack. Carefully remove the lids with a sharp knife and scoop out any uncooked mixture from the centre.

For the sauce, melt the butter in a saucepan and add the flour and cook for a minute. Blend in the milk and bring to the boil, stirring until thickened, add the remaining ingredients and cook gently for about 3 minutes.

Fill into the pastry cases, replace the lids and reheat for about 15 minutes in a moderate oven when required.

English soused herrings   *Serves 4*

Best served cold, they will keep in the refrigerator for a couple of days.

4 herrings	*1 bay leaf*
Salt and pepper	*6 cloves*
1 small onion, thinly sliced	*150 ml (5 fl oz) malt vinegar*
1 tsp peppercorns	*150 ml (5 fl oz) water*

Heat the oven to 180° C (350° F), gas mark 4.

Clean the herrings and remove the heads and tails. Season the flesh well with salt and pepper and roll up each fish, place close together in an ovenproof dish, add the remaining ingredients, cover with a lid or piece of foil and bake in the oven for 1 hour, remove and leave to cool in the dish.

Smoked haddock soufflé   *Serves 3–4*

We like this as a supper dish with slices of fresh brown bread and butter.

225 g (8 oz) smoked haddock   *50 g (2 oz) flour*
300 ml (10 fl oz) milk   *4 large eggs, separated*
50 g (2 oz) butter   *Salt and pepper*

Heat the oven to 190° C (375° F), gas mark 5 and place a baking sheet in it.
   Well butter a 1 l (2 pt) soufflé dish with a little of the butter.
   Place the haddock in a shallow pan with the milk and simmer for 10 minutes. Strain the milk into a jug, flake the fish and remove all skin and bones.
   Melt the butter in a saucepan and stir in the flour and cook for a minute, and then add the milk and bring to the boil, stirring until thickened. Cook for 2 minutes, then remove the pan from the heat and beat in the egg yolks, stir in the fish and season well.
   Whisk the egg whites with a rotary or electric hand whisk until stiff but not dry. Stir 1 heaped tbsp into the fish mixture and then carefully fold in the remainder.
   Turn into the dish and run a spoon around the edge. Place on the baking sheet in the oven and bake for 40–45 minutes until well risen and golden brown. Serve at once.

Fish cakes   *Serves 4*

Ring the changes with this basic recipe by using any variety of fish, white, smoked or canned. It is well worth taking the trouble to sieve the potatoes to get really smooth fish cakes. They also freeze well.

225 g (8 oz) cooked flaked fish   *2 hard-boiled eggs, finely chopped*
450 g (1 lb) potatoes, cooked and sieved   *(optional)*
1 level tbsp fresh chopped parsley   *1 egg, beaten*
Salt and pepper   *Browned breadcrumbs*

Place the fish, potatoes, parsley, seasoning (and hard-boiled egg if used) in a bowl and mix well. Shape into a roll and then cut into 8 even sized slices.
   Coat the fish cakes in beaten egg and browned breadcrumbs and put in a cool place until required.
   Melt a little fat in a frying pan and fry the fish cakes for about 4 minutes on each side. Lift out and drain on kitchen paper and serve with a home-made tomato sauce.

To freeze: open freeze, then pack into a container, cover and label. To serve: thaw at room temperature for 3–4 hours and then cook as above.

FISH FOR SPECIAL OCCASIONS

Salmon gently poached and served cold with cucumber mayonnaise, or Dover sole grilled with melted butter – these fish dishes are classic in their simplicity. Their success depends on ingredients of superlative quality, and these cost money. Good fish today is as expensive as good meat, and just as rewarding.

Use it for a special lunch or supper, or for a gala dinner; it can be an attractive party dish in its own right, and an interesting alternative to meat.

Take trouble to present it attractively. You can save money by using lemon sole rather than the very expensive Dover sole, but do make sure that it is dressed for the occasion. Trout will stand in for salmon at a festive dinner. Buy it fresh if you can, or frozen if you can't, and serve it fried with almonds or baked with a hollandaise sauce. Cooking times are not long and the accompaniments are half the battle.

Crab is usually sold ready cooked. Dressed crab takes a certain amount of preparation but it is easy to serve for a summer lunch or a very special picnic. It looks terrific, too.

Sole with taramasalata   *Serves 2*

Use lemon sole for this recipe rather than the very expensive Dover sole which to my mind is best served simply grilled with butter.

2 large or 4 small fillets of lemon sole
85 g (3 oz) jar taramasalata (smoked
 cod's roe pâté)
300 ml (10 fl oz) milk
550 g (1¼ lb) potatoes, boiled and
 mashed

A little butter and milk
25 g (1 oz) butter
25 g (1 oz) flour
2–3 tbsp single cream
Salt and pepper
Small sprigs of parsley to garnish

Remove any dark skin from the sole and spread the skin side of each fillet with the taramasalata and roll up with the filling inside. Place in a shallow pan, pour the milk over, cover and poach gently for about 15 minutes or until the fish is cooked.

Meanwhile season the potato, add a little butter and enough milk to make it a pipeable consistency, then pipe or fork the potato into a border around the edge of a shallow ovenproof dish.

Carefully lift the fillets from the pan with a slotted spoon and place in the centre of the potato and keep warm.

Melt the butter in a small pan and stir in the flour and cook for a minute. Add the cooking liquor from the fish and bring to the boil, stirring; cook for 2 minutes to thicken the sauce. Season well and then remove the sauce from the heat and stir in the cream. Spoon over the fish and garnish with small sprigs of parsley.

Trout with almonds   *Serves 4 (See cover photograph)*

Use flaked or split almonds for this recipe – they go further than whole almonds. You may well have a good source of supply for trout near you as trout farms are becoming more popular. We have one near us and I am able to choose small 150 g (5 oz) fish for the children and 225 g (8 oz) ones for the grown-ups.

4 trout
Seasoned flour
75 g (3 oz) butter

50 g (2 oz) flaked almonds
Lemon wedges and parsley to garnish

Wash the trout under running water to remove any loose blood. If the trout has not been cleaned slit along the belly with a sharp knife and remove the gut; wash thoroughly (and remove the eyes), dry on kitchen paper.

Coat the trout in flour. Melt 50 g (2 oz) of the butter in a large frying pan and fry the fish for 7–8 minutes, turning once. Lift out of the pan and arrange on a warm serving dish.

Add the remaining butter to the pan with the almonds and fry quickly until golden brown, stirring continuously. Pour the almond and butter mixture over the trout and then garnish with lemon wedges and small sprigs of parsley and serve at once.

Baked trout with hollandaise sauce   *Serves 4*

You could use a small salmon instead of trout. It is difficult to get large trout from fish shops and freezer centres, but no problem if you have a trout farm nearby. Remember fresh, cleaned, uncooked trout or salmon freeze well.

Butter
1·1 kg (2½ lb) trout, cleaned and the
 head left on

Salt and ground black pepper
Juice of 1 lemon
Parsley to garnish

Heat the oven to 180° C (350° F), gas mark 4. Butter well a shallow ovenproof dish and lay the fish in it. Season inside and out and sprinkle with lemon juice, dot with a little butter and cover the dish with foil.

Bake in the oven for about 35 minutes or until the flesh can easily be lifted up and looks opaque when a knife is inserted down the back bone. Serve in the dish, garnished with a sprig of parsley and hollandaise sauce.

Hollandaise sauce

50 ml (2 fl oz) cider or wine vinegar
6 peppercorns
½ bay leaf
1 blade mace

3 egg yolks
100 g (4 oz) unsalted butter
¼ tsp salt
Pinch white pepper

Put the vinegar, peppercorns, bay leaf and mace in a pan and simmer until the vinegar is reduced to 1 tbsp. Put the egg yolks in the blender, add the strained vinegar and blend on maximum speed for a few seconds. Just before serving bring the butter to boiling point in a pan, switch blender to maximum speed for a few seconds, and then slowly pour on the boiling butter; blend until thick, add seasoning and pour into a warmed sauce boat and serve at once.

Crab and egg mousse   *Serves 4–5*

An easy to make lunch or light supper dish for when you have guests; serve on a warm day with hot brown rolls and a crisp green salad.

25 g (1 oz) butter
25 g (1 oz) flour
300 ml (10 fl oz) milk
1 chicken stock cube
12·5 g (½ oz) gelatine
1 tbsp lemon juice

150 ml (5 fl oz) mayonnaise
175 g (6 oz) flaked crab meat
2 hard-boiled eggs, chopped
150 ml (5 fl oz) whipping cream
Tomato slices to garnish

Melt the butter in a small saucepan and add the flour and cook for a minute. Add the milk and the stock cube and bring to the boil, stirring until the sauce has thickened and the stock cube dissolved, simmer for two minutes and then remove from the heat. Lightly sprinkle on the gelatine and stir until dissolved. Turn into a bowl and leave to cool until luke warm.

   Add the lemon juice, mayonnaise, crab meat and eggs and mix lightly and season to taste.

   Lightly whip the cream and fold into the mixture, turn into a shallow 1 l (2 pt) dish and put in the refrigerator and leave to set; decorate the top with tomato slices.

Salmon cutlets with cucumber mayonnaise   *Serves 6*

Serve this for a summer dinner party, when salmon is at its best, with buttered new potatoes and a green or mixed salad.

6 salmon steaks
600 ml (1 pt) water
1 tbsp vinegar
1 rounded tsp salt

300 ml (10 fl oz) mayonnaise
150 ml (5 fl oz) soured cream
¼ cucumber, peeled and finely diced

Wash steaks and trim if necessary.

   Put the water, vinegar and salt in a frying pan and bring to the boil. Place the salmon steaks in the pan, lower the heat and poach very gently for 5–10 minutes – the length of time will vary with the thickness of the salmon steak. Lift out very carefully and put on a wire rack and leave to drain and become quite cold; it is a good idea to put a large dish under the rack to catch any drips.

Place on a serving dish and garnish with lettuce and watercress.

Put the mayonnaise in a bowl and stir in the soured cream and cucumber and mix lightly. Turn into a small dish and serve with the salmon.

Dressed crab   *Serves 4*

This is a lovely thing to do in the summer for a light lunch or supper with friends. It takes a little time but always looks good, and once done is so easy to serve with salads, crusty rolls or French bread and a dish of mayonnaise.

1·1 kg (2½ lb) crab, cooked
Salt
Freshly ground black pepper
White wine vinegar

1–2 tbsp fresh white breadcrumbs
A little lemon juice
Fresh chopped parsley

Place the crab on a board and twist off the legs and two large claws. Twist off the pincers and crack each claw open with a claw cracker, hammer or the handle of a heavy knife. Empty the white meat into a bowl and use the handle of a teaspoon or a skewer to scrape all the white meat from the crevices in the claws. Set the small legs aside for decoration or, if they are large, crack them open with a hammer and extract the white meat with a skewer.

Place the crab on its back and firmly pull the body (to which the legs were attached) away from the shell. Remove the greyish-white stomach sac which lies behind the head in the shell and the grey feathered gills (known as dead men's fingers) and discard the lot.

Using a spoon, gently scrape the soft brown meat from the shell and put in another bowl until required.

Cut the body part in two and pick out the white meat left in the leg sockets. Using the handle of a knife, tap and trim away the shell along the natural dark line around the rim. Scrub inside the shell and wash thoroughly under cold water, dry and, if liked, brush with a little oil and set aside.

Finely chop the white meat and season to taste with salt, black pepper and a few drops of white wine vinegar.

Mix the brown meat with the breadcrumbs, seasoning and a little lemon juice; stir in a little chopped parsley.

Put the white meat on each side of the shell and the brown meat down the centre.

ROASTS

Sunday lunch is the high spot of the week. The whole family is assembled, with plenty of time to enjoy the food – and nothing much to do afterwards but digest it. At least that is the traditional view. Things may be a little different now and we may look back on regular roast beef and Yorkshire pudding with nostalgia, but the fact remains that the roast, whether it is beef, lamb or poultry, is in the good, comforting tradition of family cooking, the centrepiece of the old-fashioned lunch.

But there is no need to be either traditional or old-fashioned in the way you cook and serve your roast. There are endless varieties of roast chicken – for example try it with tomato and mushroom sauce. Consider a joint of bacon – honey-glazed gammon with apple for a special dinner – or there is pork with an interesting stuffing, crown roast or a saddle of lamb for the big occasion.

Where you can, cook the vegetables in the oven along with the roast; it makes serving easier, you save fuel, and it all tastes better anyway.

Garlic lamb   *Serves 8*

Very garlicky and easy to carve. The joy of this roast is that the whole lot goes into the oven at the same time. Just serve with a tossed green salad.

1 small shoulder of lamb, boned
Salt and pepper
350 g (12 oz) sausagemeat
50 g (2 oz) fresh brown breadcrumbs
2 tbsp freshly chopped herbs

Finely grated rind of half a lemon
2 cloves garlic
900 g (2 lb) potatoes
350 g (12 oz) onions
300 ml (10 fl oz) stock

Heat the oven to 180° C (350° F), gas mark 4.

Open the lamb out flat and season well.

Blend the sausagemeat, breadcrumbs, herbs and lemon rind together and put into the cavity in the shoulder. Press back into shape and secure with string or skewers. Peel the garlic and cut into thin slivers and insert them into the lamb.

Peel the potatoes and cut into thick slices. Peel and thinly slice the onions, mix with the potatoes, place in a shallow ovenproof dish and season well. Put the lamb on top, pour the stock over.

Cover with a piece of foil and roast in the oven for 30 minutes for each 450 g (1 lb) and 30 minutes over. After the first hour remove the foil, baste the meat and vegetables and then continue cooking.

Serve in the dish that it is cooked in.

Roast chicken with tomato and mushroom sauce   *Serves 6*
(*See cover photograph*)

A lovely way to serve chicken when tomatoes are plentiful in the garden.

1·8 kg (4 lb) oven-ready chicken
Butter
150 ml (5 fl oz) water
150 ml (5 fl oz) dry white wine or cider
40 g (1½ oz) butter

1 large onion, sliced
40 g (1½ oz) flour
Salt and pepper
100 g (4 oz) button mushrooms, sliced
450 g (1 lb) tomatoes, peeled and
  quartered

Heat the oven to 190° C (375° F), gas mark 5.

Remove the giblets from the chicken and keep the liver on one side. Put the chicken in a roasting tin with the giblets, water and wine or cider, season well and spread a very little butter over the breast of the chicken and cover with a piece of greaseproof paper.

Roast in the oven, basting occasionally for 1½–1¾ hours or until the chicken is tender. When cooked lift out and place on a warm serving dish and keep warm.

Melt the butter in a saucepan and add the onion and cook gently for about 8 minutes or until tender, add the chopped chicken liver and fry for about 2 minutes. Stir in the the flour and cook for a minute and then strain in the cooking liquor from the chicken and bring to the boil, stirring until thickened. Add the mushrooms and tomatoes and simmer gently for 3–4 minutes. Taste and check seasoning and spoon a little sauce around the chicken and serve the remainder separately.

Duchesse potatoes are very nice served with this dish.

Honey-glazed gammon   *Serves 8–10*

This is ideal for a family celebration, served either hot or cold.

1·8 kg (4 lb) gammon joint
450 ml (15 fl oz) apple juice
1 onion
Freshly ground black pepper
2 tbsp honey

3 Cox's apples
50 g (2 oz) demerara sugar
25 g (1 oz) butter
2 tbsp oil

Soak the gammon for 12 hours in cold water, then drain. Place in a saucepan, pour the apple juice over, slice the onion and add with the black pepper.

Cover and simmer for 20 minutes for each 450 g (1 lb) plus 20 minutes over.

Remove gammon from the pan and leave to cool slightly.

Remove the skin and score fat diagonally in diamond shapes and put in a shallow ovenproof dish. Brush with honey and bake in the oven at 220° C (425° F), gas mark 7 for about 15 minutes or until a rich golden brown.

Core the apples and cut into rings, leaving the skin on. Toss in the sugar. Heat the butter and oil together in a pan and fry the apple rings, turning once, until they are a golden syrupy brown.

Place the gammon on a dish surrounded with apple rings.

Pot-roast beef   *Serves 8*

Pot-roasted slices of beef are served in a tomato sauce.

25 g (1 oz) dripping
1·3 kg (3 lb) piece brisket of beef
3 medium onions, sliced
397 g (14 oz) can peeled tomatoes
1 level tsp mixed dried herbs
Salt and pepper
25 g (1 oz) cornflour
1 tbsp water

Heat the dripping in a saucepan and add the beef and quickly fry to brown all over, lift out and put on one side. Then add the onions to the fat in the pan and fry quickly for 3 minutes.

Drain off any excess fat and then add the tomatoes, herbs and seasoning to the pan and put the meat back on top of the vegetables. Cover with a tight fitting lid and simmer very gently for about 2¼ hours or until the meat is tender; allow about 35 minutes for each 450 g (1 lb) and 35 minutes over.

Lift out the meat and place on a warm serving dish. Blend the cornflour with the water in a small bowl and then add a spoon of the tomato mixture, stir into the saucepan and bring to the boil, stirring continually until the sauce has thickened; simmer for 3 minutes, taste and check seasoning and then serve in a sauce boat with the beef.

Chinese pork   *Serves 6–8*

The long, slow cooking results in an absolutely delicious, succulent, tender dish. Serve with bean sprouts and light fluffy rice.

1·8 kg (4 lb) hand or knuckle of pork   *12 tbsp boiling water*
6 tbsp soy sauce   *1 tbsp sugar*
6 tbsp dry sherry

Ask the butcher to bone the pork but leave the skin on.

Heat the oven to 180° C (350° F), gas mark 4.

Put the pork in a flameproof casserole, add the remaining ingredients and place over a medium heat and bring to the boil. Cook for 2–3 minutes, turning the pork. Cover the casserole and put in the oven and leave to cook for 3 hours, turning the pork every half hour, or until the pork is very tender and can easily be cut into bite-sized pieces.

The skin of the pork should be treated as jelly and is excellent eaten with rice. The gravy is one of the high points of Chinese cookery.

Crown roast of lamb   *Serves 6–8*

A crown roast consists of two joints of best end of neck chined and then tied or sewn together back to back; it is not difficult to do but your butcher will always do this for you if you give him warning.

2 joints best end of lamb

Stuffing
25 g (1 oz) dried apricots, soaked
½ cooking apple
62 g (2½ oz) fresh white breadcrumbs
1 tbsp chopped walnuts
Grated rind of half a lemon
25 g (1 oz) melted butter
Salt and pepper

Prepare a moderate oven 180° C (350° F), gas mark 4.

Have the chine joints of meat removed by the butcher. Trim the tips of the bones of surplus fat so that they stick out for about 2·5 cm (1 in). Using thin string and a trussing needle sew the two joints together back to back with the cutlet joint curving up and outwards to form the shape of the crown.

Place the joint in a roasting tin, season well and wrap a small piece of foil around the top of each bone to prevent it burning during cooking. Now prepare the stuffing: using a pair of scissors, snip the apricots, into small pieces; peel, core and chop the apple and blend with the apricots, breadcrumbs, nuts, lemon rind and melted butter, season to taste and then put into the centre of the crown.

Put a little dripping in the pan with the meat and roast for about 1½ hours or for about 25 minutes for each 450 g (1 lb).

To serve, remove the string and pieces of foil from the lamb and place on a warm serving dish and put a cutlet frill on each bone.

If liked, the dish may be garnished with green peas and carrot dice or apricot halves filled with mint jelly.

To carve, cut down between the bones and serve two chops per person.

Roast saddle of lamb   *Serves 6*

This is an expensive joint but well worth having for a special occasion.

Saddle of lamb, weight as required	*2 sprigs rosemary*
50 g (2 oz) butter	*Salt and pepper*

Gravy

2 tbsp meat fat	*1 tsp redcurrant jelly*
25 g (1 oz) flour	*Salt and pepper*
300 ml (10 fl oz) stock	*2 tbsp sherry*

Heat the oven to 190° C (375° F), gas mark 5.

Ask your butcher to cut the weight of the saddle you would like; for 6 take a saddle which weighs 2–3·4 kg (4½–7 lb). This cut is two loins together from ribs to tail; the kidneys are sometimes sent with the saddle and may be roasted and served with the joint, a slice being served with each portion.

Roast the joint in a large meat tin allowing 25 minutes for each 450 g (1 lb) and 25 minutes over; if you like your lamb rare cook it for 20 minutes for each 450 g (1 lb). Before putting it in the oven, spread the joint with butter, tuck the rosemary under the joint to give added flavour and season well. Start roasting the joint with a piece of foil over it which should be removed after 30 minutes. Lift out and place on a serving dish, keep warm.

To make the gravy: strain off all but 2 tbsp of the fat from the pan, add the flour to the pan and cook on top of the stove in the meat tin for a few minutes or until the flour is golden brown, stirring briskly all the time with a wooden spoon. Remove from the heat and slowly add the stock, return to the heat, bring to the boil and allow to thicken, stirring all the time. Add the redcurrant jelly, seasoning and sherry.

Serve in a sauce boat with the meat.

Tiffany pork   *Serves 8–10*

A boned pork joint with a really interesting stuffing. By no means a budget dish – ideal for a dinner party when the pork can easily be served in view.

1·8 kg (4 lb) loin of pork, chined
225 g (8 oz) packet chopped spinach, cooked
225 g (8 oz) pork sausagemeat
1–2 pork kidneys, finely chopped
1 onion, finely chopped
25 g (1 oz) butter
Grated rind of 1 lemon
Salt and pepper

Heat the oven to 190° C (375° F), gas mark 5.

Carefully score the skin on the pork, and remove the bones.

Place the spinach and sausagemeat in a bowl. Put the kidneys, onion and butter in a small saucepan and cook gently for about 10 minutes, then turn into the bowl with the sausagemeat and add the lemon rind and seasoning and mix well.

Place the pork on the board skin side down and put some of the stuffing down the centre of the meat, then roll the meat over and tie securely with fine string so that the stuffing is in the centre of the roll; put in as much stuffing as is possible and place the remainder in a small buttered dish. Place in the roasting tin and cook the meat for about 2½ hours. Add the dish of stuffing for the last 30 minutes of the cooking time.

Serve with apple sauce and a gravy made from juices in the pan.

Any leftover meat may be served the following day with a selection of salads.

Classic roast turkey

When cooking a very large bird at a lower temperature it will be necessary to cook the sausages, bacon and potatoes for a little longer. You can usually reckon on getting 20 servings from a 5·4–6·3 kg (12–14 lb) turkey.

If using a frozen bird, thaw completely according to the directions given on the wrapping.

Check the weight of the bird with the stuffings and then calculate the cooking time. Heat the oven.

Put a large piece of foil in the roasting tin and lift the turkey onto it and season well. Wrap the foil loosely over the turkey with the fold at the top. Place the turkey on a shelf just below the centre of the oven or lower according to the size of the bird.

To brown the turkey undo the foil and rub the breast and legs with butter.

Cook with the foil open for the last 1¼ hours of the time for a large bird and for about 50 minutes for a small bird that is under 4·5 kg (10 lb).

Place the sausages in a greased roasting tin and cook above the turkey when the foil has been opened. Add the bacon rolls on skewers on top of the sausages 30 minutes before the end of the cooking time.

Roast potatoes may be cooked for the last 1½–1¾ hours above the turkey. Bring prepared potatoes to the boil in a pan of water on the stove starting from cold. Drain thoroughly. Heat oil or fat in a meat tin in the oven, then add the potatoes, turning during roasting.

2·7–3·2 kg (6–7 lb)	3–3½ hours at 180° C (350° F), gas mark 4.
3·6–4·5 kg (8–10 lb)	3½–4 hours at 180° C (350° F), gas mark 4.
5·0–6·9 kg (11–15 lb)	4–4½ hours at 180° C (350° F), gas mark 4.
7·2–9·0 kg (16–20 lb)	5–5½ hours at 160° C (325° F), gas mark 3.

Nightingale's veal   *Serves 8–10*

Try for Sunday lunch for a change. This is more popular with grown-ups;
I find that children prefer lamb and mint sauce.

Stuffing
25 g (1 oz) butter
1 onion, chopped
4 rashers streaky bacon, chopped
100 g (4 oz) fresh white breadcrumbs
Grated rind of 1 lemon

1 tsp chopped fresh lemon thyme
1 tbsp chopped fresh parsley
Salt and pepper
1 egg, beaten

1·3 kg (3 lb) boned shoulder or
  breast of veal

Juice of 1 lemon
50 g (2 oz) butter

Gravy
25 g (1 oz) dripping
25 g (1 oz) flour

5 tbsp dry vermouth
150 ml (5 fl oz) stock

Heat the oven to 200° C (400° F), gas mark 6.

First make the stuffing: melt the butter in a pan, add the onion and
bacon and fry gently for 5 minutes so that all the fat runs out of the bacon.
Remove from the heat and stir in the remaining ingredients and mix
thoroughly. Spread the veal out on a board, spread with the stuffing and
then roll up and tie securely with fine string. Place on a piece of foil on a
meat tin and pour the lemon juice over, dot with the butter and then
lightly seal the foil and roast in the oven for 2 hours, allowing 30 minutes
for each 450 g (1 lb) and 30 minutes over. Open up the foil for the last 30
minutes of the cooking time to allow the veal to brown.

For the gravy: melt the dripping in a pan, add the flour and then cook
gently for at least 5 minutes until pale golden brown. Remove from the
heat and add the juices from the meat, vermouth and stock, and season
well. Return to the heat and bring to the boil, stirring, until thickened and
then simmer for 2–3 minutes and serve with the meat.

CHICKEN, DUCK AND GAME

All keen cooks look for variety in their menus. It isn't difficult to get away from conventional chicken, roast, boiled or casseroled. Chicken is on everyone's menu. It is good value for money and the meat is tender. Its rather bland taste makes it a good background for other flavourings, spices, herbs, vegetables. This is one of the great advantages of chicken; you can serve it in literally hundreds of different ways, cook it how you like and flavour it according to your, and your family's taste.

Duck and game, on the other hand, have their own distinctive character and their traditional accompanying flavours: orange with duck – try it with ginger orange marmalade sauce – redcurrant jelly with jugged hare.

Game is not all grouse and roast pheasant, delightful as these are. An elderly pheasant, long past roasting, will casserole slowly and beautifully and come out as tender as spring chicken. And have you tried casserole of pigeons for a comparatively inexpensive dish? Don't neglect the humble rabbit either.

Chicken extraordinaire   *Serves 6*

This colourful dish is ideal for a cold buffet.

1·5 kg (3½ lb) chicken
1 onion, sliced
1 carrot, sliced

1 bay leaf
Salt and pepper

Sauce
190 g (6¾ oz) can pimentos
1 onion, chopped finely
1 tbsp tomato purée
1 tsp sugar

Salt and freshly ground black pepper
1 clove garlic, crushed
300 ml (10 fl oz) mayonnaise

Watercress and tomatoes to garnish

Put the chicken in a large pan with the onion and carrot and pour on sufficient water to cover. Add the bay leaf and season well, cover the pan and simmer for about 1½ hours or until tender. Remove the pan from the heat and leave to cool in the liquid. Then lift out the chicken and remove the meat from the bones, discarding all the skin. Cut the meat into fork sized pieces and place on a serving dish.

Meanwhile prepare the sauce: drain the pimentos and put 2 tbsp of the brine in a small saucepan. Cut a quarter of one of the pimentos into neat strips and put on one side for garnish. Put the remaining pimentos into the pan with the onion, purée, sugar, seasoning and garlic, cover and simmer for 5 minutes. Then mix in a blender until quite smooth, or sieve, leave to become quite cold and then stir into the mayonnaise, a little at a time.

Taste and adjust seasoning if necessary and then spoon over the chicken. Decorate the dish with small sprigs of watercress and quartered tomatoes.

Arrange the strips of pimento over the chicken.

Easy spiced chicken   *Serves 4*

Very simple – just marinate the chicken overnight, and next day bake without frying first. If liked you may remove the chicken skin first.

4 chicken joints	*3 tbsp mango chutney*
3 tbsp oil	*2 tbsp soft brown sugar*
3 tbsp tomato ketchup	*1 tsp anchovy essence*
1 tbsp Worcestershire sauce	*Watercress to garnish*

Lay the chicken in a single layer in a shallow ovenproof dish.

Mix the oil, ketchup, Worcestershire sauce, chutney, sugar and anchovy essence together and then spoon over the chicken and leave to stand in the fridge overnight or for at least 6–8 hours.

Heat the oven to 190° C (375° F), gas mark 5 and bake the chicken for 40 minutes, basting regularly so that the sauce adheres to the chicken. If the chicken starts to brown too much cover with a lid of foil. Garnish with small sprigs of watercress and serve at once.

Coq au vin   *Serves 6*

A very tasty way of serving chicken, good enough for entertaining as it may be made in advance.

1·5–1·8 kg (3½–4 lb) roasting chicken	*350 g (12 oz) button onions, peeled*
Salt and pepper	*1 clove garlic, crushed*
1 bay leaf and a sprig of parsley	*300 ml (10 fl oz) red wine*
40 g (1½ oz) seasoned flour	*300 ml (10 fl oz) chicken stock*
25 g (1 oz) butter	*1 tbsp tomato purée*
1 tbsp oil	*175 g (6 oz) button mushrooms*
100 g (4 oz) piece of streaky bacon	

Remove the giblets from the chicken. Cut the legs and the wings from the chicken and then trim the backbone from the carcass and split the breast in half lengthwise to make six joints in all; take the skin from each piece of chicken.

Put the giblets, backbone and skin in a saucepan with salt, pepper, bay leaf and parsley and sufficient water to cover, then bring to the boil, reduce the heat and simmer for about 40 minutes to make a good stock. Strain off and keep 300 ml (10 fl oz) on one side for the recipe; any spare may be used for soups or sauces.

Heat the oven to 180° C (350° F), gas mark 4.

Coat the chicken joints in the flour. Heat the butter and oil in a large frying pan and add the chicken and fry until brown on all sides, then lift out with a slotted spoon and place in an ovenproof casserole.

Remove the rind and bone from the bacon and cut into 1·25 cm (½ in) strips and add to the pan with the onions and fry quickly for 4–5 minutes, lift out and add to the casserole.

Stir the remaining flour into the fat in the pan and cook for 2 minutes. Add the red wine and chicken stock and bring to the boil, stirring until thickened; stir in the tomato purée and season well. Pour the sauce over the chicken, cover the casserole and cook in the oven for 45 minutes.

Add the mushrooms and continue cooking for a further 15 minutes or until the chicken is tender. Taste and check seasoning before serving.

Pigeons paysanne   *Serves 4*

The cooking time varies with the age of the pigeons; long, slow cooking is best. Cook until the thigh joints of the birds are tender when pierced with a fine skewer. Add the cream just before serving and do not reboil.

12 button onions	*600 ml (1 pt) stock*
50 g (2 oz) butter	*1 sprig lemon thyme*
4 pigeons	*Salt and pepper*
2 sticks celery, chopped	*3–4 tbsp soured cream*
25 g (1 oz) flour	*2 tbsp brandy*

Peel the onions, leaving them whole. Melt the butter in a large pan and brown the pigeons and onions all over, lift out with a slotted spoon and put on one side. Add the celery to the pan and fry for 2 minutes, stir in the flour and cook for a minute, then gradually blend in the stock and bring to the boil, stirring until thickened. Add the thyme and seasoning and then return the pigeons and onions to the pan, cover and simmer gently for 1½ hours or until the pigeons are tender.

Lift out the pigeons and place on a warm serving dish.

Blend the soured cream with the brandy and add 2–3 tbsp of the sauce, then stir all of it back into the pan. Taste and check seasoning and spoon over the pigeons, put the onions and celery around the birds with a little sauce and serve the remainder separately.

Duck with ginger orange marmalade sauce   *Serves 4*

The ginger marmalade makes an interesting glaze; serve with an orange salad and watercress.

4 duck portions	*12·5 g (½ oz) butter*
Salt and pepper	*Juice of 1 orange*
1 tbsp soy sauce	*1 rounded tsp cornflour*
2 rounded tbsp ginger marmalade	*150 ml (5 fl oz) stock*
1 small onion, very finely chopped	

Heat the oven to 190° C (375° F), gas mark 5. Prick the skin of the duck all over with a sharp knife and place on a trivet in a roasting tin and roast for 30 minutes. Remove the duck from the oven and drain off all the fat from the tin. Combine the sauce with the marmalade and coat the duck with half of the mixture, return to the oven for a further 20 minutes or until tender. Test to see if the duck is done by piercing the thigh with a skewer – the juices should run clear, not pink.

Meanwhile cook the onion in the butter in a small pan until pale golden brown. Add the orange juice and the remaining glaze mixture. Blend the cornflour with the stock and stir into the pan, bring to the boil, stirring until it has thickened and then simmer for 5 minutes. Taste and check seasoning. Place duck on a warm serving dish and serve the sauce separately.

Orange salad

3 large oranges	50 ml (2 fl oz) oil
½ tsp made mustard	1 tbsp white wine or cider vinegar
1 tsp caster sugar	1 tbsp orange juice
½ tsp salt	

Peel one orange very thinly, removing just the outside zest. Shred this finely and simmer in a little water for 3–4 minutes; drain. With a small, sharp knife remove the peel and outside white pith from the oranges and slice into very thin slices on a plate to catch the juice. Arrange the slices in a dish and scatter with the orange peel.

Make a dressing by mixing the mustard, sugar and salt together and slowly working in the oil, and then the vinegar and orange juice saved from the oranges.

Spoon the dressing over the orange slices and leave to marinade in a cool place for at least an hour before serving.

Chicken with fresh herbs   *Serves 4*

Make for a special family supper dish; it is best made and then served at once so that the herbs have a good colour and flavour.

4 chicken breasts	100 g (4 oz) streaky bacon
Seasoned flour	150 ml (5 fl oz) dry white wine or cider
1 tbsp oil	150 ml (5 fl oz) chicken stock
25 g (1 oz) butter	2 tbsp chopped mixed fresh herbs

Remove the skin from chicken breasts and coat each in a little seasoned flour. Heat the oil and butter in a large pan and then fry the chicken to lightly brown on all sides.

Remove rind and bone from the bacon and cut into thin strips, add to the pan and fry for 2 minutes. Stir in the wine, stock and herbs, cover the pan and simmer gently for about 25 minutes or until the chicken is tender, turning once.

Lift out the chicken and arrange on a warm serving dish and keep warm. Increase the heat under the pan and boil the sauce rapidly for a few minutes until it has reduced and thickened slightly. Check seasoning, spoon over the chicken and serve at once.

Spicy chicken   *Serves 6*

This dish is an ideal way of serving cooked chicken or turkey. The sauce is spicy and colourful and just needs to be served with plain boiled rice or noodles and a tossed green salad.

2 onions, chopped
50 g (2 oz) butter
2 level tbsp flour
1 level tsp chilli powder
397 g (14 oz) can peeled tomatoes
1 tbsp Worcestershire sauce
2 tbsp tomato pureé
450 ml (15 fl oz) chicken stock

1 tsp sugar
1 bay leaf
Salt and pepper
450 g (1 lb) cooked chicken or turkey
432 g (15 oz) can kidney beans, drained
200 g (7 oz) can red peppers, drained and cut in strips

Fry the onions in the butter for about 5 minutes and then stir in the flour and chilli powder and cook for 2 minutes. Add the tomatoes, Worcestershire sauce, tomato purée, stock, sugar, bay leaf and seasoning and bring to the boil, stirring until the sauce has thickened and come to the boil. Partially cover the pan and simmer for 30 minutes; remove bay leaf.

Stir in the chicken, kidney beans and red pepper and reheat, then taste and check seasoning. Turn into a warm serving dish and serve piping hot with rice or noodles.

Chicken with lemon and parsley   *Serves 6–8*

If you can get a boiling fowl for this recipe it is best. Ideal for a family get together, particularly if the older folk come too.

1·8 kg (4 lb) boiling fowl with giblets
Thinly peeled rind of 1 large lemon
2 sprigs of parsley
2 onions, quartered

1 carrot, quartered
Bouquet garni
Salt and pepper

Sauce
40 g (1½ oz) butter
40 g (1½ oz) flour
150 ml (5 fl oz) milk

Juice of 1 large lemon
Chopped fresh parsley to garnish

Rinse the fowl with cold water. Put the giblets, rind of half the lemon and a sprig of parsley inside the bird and put in a large casserole. Add the remaining lemon rind and a second sprig of parsley, onions, carrot, bouquet garni and seasoning. Pour in sufficient hot water to cover the bird, cover and put in the oven at 160° C (325° F), gas mark 3 and cook gently for 2–4 hours, depending on the age of the bird, or until it is tender. To test remove the lid and raise the drumstick to see if the joint of the leg is loose.

Remove the bird from the casserole and discard the giblets, lemon rind and parsley inside. Set aside on a serving dish and keep warm while making the sauce.

Skim the fat off the stock and strain off 300 ml (10 fl oz) and set aside; the remainder may be used to make soup.

Melt the butter in a saucepan and stir in the flour and cook for 2 minutes. Remove the pan from the heat and gradually stir in the milk and stock. Return the pan to the heat and bring the sauce to the boil, stirring constantly. Remove the pan from the heat and add the lemon juice, taste and season. Pour the sauce over the chicken and sprinkle with parsley.

Cider chicken   *Serves 6*

This is a colourful dish, with a lovely flavour and so easy to serve.

1·5 kg (3½ lb) chicken
300 ml (10 fl oz) extra dry cider
2 onions, chopped
Black pepper
Salt

Milk
50 g (2 oz) butter
50 g (2 oz) flour
200 g (7 oz) can red peppers, drained
and sliced

Put the chicken and giblets in a small roasting tin or casserole. Add the cider and onions and season with black pepper and salt. Cover with foil or a lid and cook at 180° C (350° F), gas mark 4 for 20 minutes for each 450 g (1 lb) and 20 minutes over, i.e. about 1½ hours. Test to see if the chicken is done by piercing the thick part of the leg with a skewer; if the juices come out clear the bird is cooked; if the juices are pink continue cooking for a little longer. Lift out the chicken and leave to cool, strain off the remaining liquid in the tin, skim off the fat and make up to 750 ml (1¼ pt) with milk.

Save the chicken liver with the bird and remove all the meat from the chicken, cutting it into good-sized pieces. Chop the liver. Use the carcass and giblets to make stock for soup on another occasion.

Melt the butter in a saucepan, add the flour and cook for 2 minutes. Stir in the stock and milk and bring to the boil, stirring until thickened. Add the red pepper and season well, using lots of freshly ground black pepper.

Stir in the meat and heat through until piping hot. Turn into a dish and serve.

Jugged hare *Serves 6–10*

Excellent, but first you have to like it! I find it best not to add the blood to the hare at the end. In nine cases out of ten it seems to curdle the sauce because one ends up by reheating it over the fierce heat.

1 hare, jointed and trimmed	1 mace blade
50 g (2 oz) bacon fat	Salt and pepper
1 celery stalk, chopped	1 l (1¾ pt) water
2 large onions, each stuck with 2 cloves	50 g (2 oz) butter mixed to a paste with
6 peppercorns	50 g (2 oz) flour
Finely pared rind of half a lemon	150 ml (5 fl oz) port or Madeira
Pinch of cayenne pepper	2 tbsp redcurrant jelly
1 sprig of thyme	Fried bread croutons and
1 bay leaf	chopped parsley to garnish
2 parsley stalks	

Fry the pieces of hare in the bacon fat until they are lightly browned all over. Transfer the pieces to a casserole, add the celery, onions, peppercorns, lemon rind, cayenne, thyme, bay leaf, parsley, mace, seasoning and water. Cover tightly and cook in the oven at 160° C (325° F), gas mark 3 for 2 hours or until the hare is tender.

Transfer the hare to a serving dish. Strain the cooking liquid into a saucepan, discarding the flavourings. Gradually stir the butter and flour paste in small pieces into the liquid. When all has been added, bring to the boil and simmer gently until the sauce has thickened, stirring constantly. Stir in the port or Madeira and redcurrant jelly and boil for 2 minutes. Pour over the hare, garnish with bread croutons and sprinkle with parsley.

This dish may be frozen. Thaw in the refrigerator overnight, then put in a casserole and reheat in the oven at 160° C (325° F), gas mark 3 for about 1 hour or until hot throughout, and garnish as above.

Creamed chicken with a hint of curry *Serves 4–6*

It is essential to have grapes in this recipe – choose really large ones. Add plenty of chopped parsley to the rice or 100 g (4 oz) cooked bright green peas.

1·3 kg (3 lb) chicken with giblets	Pepper
1 small onion	300 ml (10 fl oz) boiling water
2 whole cloves	25 g (1 oz) butter
2 small carrots, sliced	1 level tbsp curry powder
1 bay leaf	25 g (1 oz) flour
1 sprig of parsley	100 g (4 oz) green grapes
1 tsp salt	5 tbsp double cream

Put the chicken and the giblets in a saucepan, add the onion stuck with cloves, the carrots, bay leaf, parsley and seasoning. Pour the water over, cover with a tight fitting lid and simmer gently for about 1 hour or until the chicken is tender. Lift out the chicken and leave to cool slightly. Strain the stock from the pan and put on one side.

Remove the flesh from the chicken and cut into neat slices or serving portions and put on a dish and keep warm.

Melt the butter in a small pan, stir in the curry powder and cook gently for 2–3 minutes. Add the flour and cook for a minute. Skim any fat from the stock and then add to the pan and bring to the boil, stirring until thickened. Halve the grapes and remove any pips. Stir into the sauce and taste and check seasoning.

Remove the pan from the heat and stir in the cream, then spoon over the chicken and serve with the rice.

This dish may be frozen, but do not add the grapes or cream; thaw overnight in the fridge, reheat gently in the oven or in a saucepan until hot, then add the grapes and cream.

Highland pheasant   *Serves 6–8*

Use aged birds for this recipe as they are casseroled until tender. It is difficult to give the exact cooking time – it really depends on the age – so the suggested cooking time is from 1–3 hours. The casserole is done when the drumstick is tender. Try pigeons done in this way too.

350 g (12 oz) chestnuts	*225 g (8 oz) onions*
3 tbsp oil	*Thinly peeled rind and juice of 1 orange*
25 g (1 oz) butter	*1 tsp redcurrant jelly*
2 casserole pheasants, each split in half	*½ tsp salt*
25 g (1 oz) flour	*Bouquet garni*
300 ml (10 fl oz) inexpensive red wine	*Ground black pepper*
300 ml (10 fl oz) chicken stock	*Sprigs of parsley to garnish*

Simmer the chestnuts in water for 30 minutes, then drain and put in cold water and skin.

Heat the oven to 160° C (325° F), gas mark 3.

Heat 2 tbsp of the oil in a pan, add the butter, then the pheasants and fry until browned, turning once. Lift out and place in a large casserole. Add the remaining oil to the pan with the chestnuts and fry until evenly browned and then drain on kitchen paper.

Add the flour to the pan and cook gently until browned. Stir in the wine and stock, bring to the boil and pour into the casserole. Peel the onions and cut in wedges, add to the casserole with the orange rind and juice, redcurrant jelly, salt, bouquet garni and black pepper. Cover and cook in the oven for 1–3 hours or until tender. Add the chestnuts about 45 minutes before the end of the cooking time.

Remove bouquet garni and orange rind. Check the seasoning and garnish the casserole with sprigs of parsley before serving.

Australian chicken   *Serves 4*

A short-cut recipe and very different – the sauce mixture becomes darker and shiny. Take care not to overcook otherwise the sauce will separate.

1 tbsp oil
4 chicken joints
4 tbsp bottled Thousand Island dressing
100 g (4 oz) apricot jam

½ packet French onion soup mix
1 clove garlic, crushed
1 tbsp Dijon mustard

Heat the oven to 180° C (350° F), gas mark 4.

Heat the oil in a frying pan and fry the chicken joints quickly to brown on both sides, then lift out and place in an ovenproof dish.

Combine the rest of the ingredients in the pan and then spoon the liquid over the chicken. Cover the dish with a piece of foil and then bake in the oven for about 1 hour or until the chicken is cooked.

Serve with a green salad and chunks of French bread.

Miracle chicken   *Serves 4–5*

A cheat recipe well worth trying; it is a very good way of using up the last of the turkey at Christmas.

25 g (1 oz) butter
25 g (1 oz) flour
300 ml (10 fl oz) milk
298 g (10½ oz) can condensed
 asparagus soup
4 tbsp sherry

150 ml (5 fl oz) double cream
Salt
Freshly ground black pepper
350 g (12 oz) cooked chicken cut in strips
280 g (10 oz) can asparagus spears
25 g (1 oz) flaked almonds, browned, to garnish

Melt the butter in a pan and stir in the flour and cook for a minute. Add the milk and bring to the boil, stirring until the sauce has thickened, blend in the condensed asparagus soup and the sherry and bring to the boil, simmer for a minute. Remove the sauce from the heat and stir in the cream, season well.

Put the chicken in a shallow ovenproof dish and arrange the drained asparagus spears on top. Pour the sauce over.

When required heat through in an oven at 160° C (325° F), gas mark 3 for 30 minutes or until piping hot and bubbling. Sprinkle with the browned flaked almonds and serve at once with rolls or slices of French bread.

Somerset chicken   *Serves 4*

Serve with buttered noodles and green beans.

4 chicken breasts	3 sticks celery, sliced
25 g (1 oz) flour	300 ml (10 fl oz) dry cider
25 g (1 oz) butter	1 level tbsp tomato purée
2 small onions, chopped	Salt and pepper

Coat the chicken in the flour. Melt the butter in a saucepan and fry the chicken until lightly brown, lift out with a slotted spoon and put on one side. Add the onion and celery to the pan and fry for a few minutes.

Stir in the remaining flour and cook for a minute, then blend in the cider and tomato purée and bring to the boil, stirring until thickened, season well.

Return the chicken breasts to the pan, cover and simmer gently for 35–40 minutes with the pan partially covered or until the chicken is tender.

This freezes well; leave to thaw at room temperature and then reheat over a gentle heat.

Chicken galantine   *Serves 10*

This takes time to do but is really worth the effort and looks very good when carved.

1·5 kg (3½ lb) chicken	½ level tsp fresh chopped thyme
350 g (12 oz) lean pork, minced	1 tsp salt
350 g (12 oz) pork sausagemeat	Plenty of ground black pepper
1 small onion, minced	100 g (4 oz) slice cooked ham
2 cloves garlic, crushed	25 g (1 oz) green stuffed olives
40 g (1½ oz) fresh breadcrumbs	A little butter
1 egg	

Bone the chicken. Make a cut along the length of the backbone and with a small, sharp knife cut the flesh away from the bones down each side. When you come to the wing knuckle cut it away with the carcass. Scrape the meat off the bone down to the first joint. Cut off there and repeat with the other side.

With the leg joint, cut away again at the carcass, but scrape the meat away from the two bones of the leg, turning the flesh inside out as you go. Carefully cut the meat away from the rest of the carcass until you can lift it out. Remove any excess lumps of fat and lay the chicken skin-side down on a board, turning the legs back into shape. Use the carcass for making soup or stock.

Heat the oven to 190° C (375° F), gas mark 5.

Mix together the pork, sausagemeat, onion, garlic, breadcrumbs, egg, thyme and salt and pepper. Spread half this mixture down the centre of the chicken. Cut the ham into 2 cm (¾ in) strips lengthwise and lay on top of the stuffing interspersed with the olives. Cover with the remaining pork mixture and wrap the chicken over. Turn over and shape to resemble a chicken, place in a roasting tin and lightly spread with butter.

Bake in the oven for 1½ hours, basting occasionally. Lift out and place on a dish to cool. When quite cold put in the refrigerator until required. Then serve sliced with various salads.

Chicken Kiev   *Serves 2*

One of Russia's most famous chicken dishes, this makes a rather special dish for two. New potatoes and a green salad are an ideal accompaniment.

Two chicken breasts, about 225 g (8 oz) | *1 clove garlic, crushed*
each with the bone | *12·5 g (½ oz) seasoned flour*
50 g (2 oz) butter | *2 eggs, beaten*
Grated rind of quarter of a lemon | *100–175 g (4–6 oz) fresh white*
2 tsp lemon juice | *breadcrumbs*
Salt and pepper | *Deep oil or fat for frying*
1 tbsp chopped parsley

Using a sharp knife carefully remove the bones from the chicken breasts; take care not to split the flesh. Put the meat between two sheets of damp greaseproof paper and bat out the chicken with a heavy knife. Then put in the refrigerator while making the filling.

Put the butter in a small bowl with the lemon rind and cream together until soft and then gradually work in the lemon juice, beating continuously. Add the seasoning, parsley and garlic and mix very thoroughly. Put the butter on a piece of non-stick parchment or foil and roll up and chill in the refrigerator.

When the butter is really hard, cut it in half and place one piece in the centre of the chicken breasts and then fold the chicken securely around the butter using some wooden cocktail sticks to hold it firmly in place. Dip the two pieces of chicken in seasoned flour, brush with beaten egg and then toss in breadcrumbs. Repeat this to get a really good coating. Put back into the refrigerator to keep cool until ready to serve.

Heat the oil or fat to 160°–180° C (325°–350° F). Put the chicken in a basket and lower into the oil and cook over a moderate heat for 12–15 minutes, so that the coating is crisp and golden brown and the chicken is tender. Care must be taken when frying the chicken so as not to fry it too quickly.

Lift out and drain on kitchen paper and then remove the cocktail sticks. When the chicken is cut the butter in the centre will have completely melted and you will find the chicken very tender.

Madeira chicken   *Serves 4*

For very special occasions, high days and holidays, so simple to make but a little rich; serve with sauté potatoes and broccoli.

4 chicken joints
50 g (2 oz) butter
225 g (8 oz) button mushrooms, sliced
150 ml (5 fl oz) double cream
4–6 tbsp Madeira or sweet sherry

2–3 tbsp chicken stock
1 level tbsp cornflour
Salt and freshly ground black pepper
Watercress to garnish

Remove the skin from the chicken joints. Heat the butter in a frying pan and add the joints, cover and cook gently for 20–25 minutes turning once. Add the mushrooms to the pan and cook for a further 5 minutes or until the chicken is tender. Lift out the chicken joints with a slotted spoon and place on a warm serving dish.

Blend the cream, Madeira, stock and cornflour together and stir into the pan and bring slowly to the boil, stirring continuously until the sauce has thickened, simmer gently for 2 minutes and then season to taste.

Spoon the sauce over the chicken and serve garnished with watercress.

Sportsman's rabbit   *Serves 4*

A very tasty way of serving rabbit; cook slowly to let all the flavours come through.

One rabbit, jointed, about 900 g (2 lb)
1 tbsp oil
25 g (1 oz) butter
2 onions, quartered
225 g (8 oz) carrots, sliced
25 g (1 oz) flour
300 ml (10 fl oz) dry cider
300 ml (10 fl oz) stock
Salt and pepper

Thoroughly wash and dry the rabbit. Heat the oil and butter in a large pan and fry the rabbit quickly to brown all over. Lift out and put on one side and then fry the onion and carrots for about 5 minutes. Stir in the flour and cook for a minute and then blend in the cider and stock and bring to the boil, stirring.

Season well and then return the rabbit joints to the pan, cover and simmer for 1½–2 hours or until the rabbit is tender. The time will vary with the age of the rabbit.

Serve the boiled potatoes and Brussels sprouts.

Roast duck with black cherry sauce   *Serves 4*

A rather special dish that could be served for a small dinner party or some special occasion, like a birthday or anniversary. Not difficult to make and may be carved in the kitchen to make serving very much easier.

1·8–2·3 kg (4½–5 lb) duckling
1 small onion, quartered
Salt and pepper
300 ml (10 fl oz) water
1435 g (15 oz) can pitted
 black cherries
2 level tbsp cornflour
3 tbsp sweet sherry

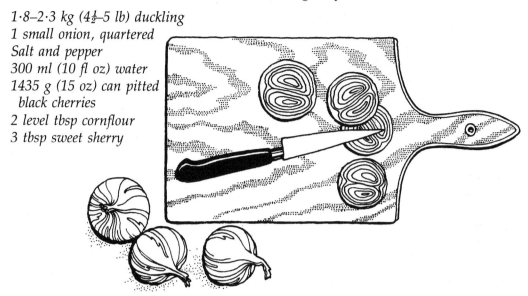

Heat the oven to 200° C (400° F), gas mark 6. Place the giblets in a small casserole with the onion, seasoning and water and place in the bottom of the oven with a tight fitting lid on the dish.

Prick the duck all over with a sharp pronged fork. Rub the salt over the duck and put on a trivet or rack in the roasting tin. Roast without basting, for about 1½ hours. Test if the duck is cooked by piercing the thickest part of the leg with a skewer and if the juices run clear the duck is done. Lift out the duck, place on a warm serving dish and rest for 5 minutes before carving.

Meanwhile, drain the juice from the cherries, place the cornflour in a small pan and stir in the cherry juice with the strained giblet stock from the oven and bring to the boil, stirring until thickened; add the sherry and seasoning to taste and then stir in the cherries. Serve in a sauce boat or dish with the duck.

Carving using sharp kitchen scissors
Cut the breast in half starting from the neck end. Cut along the length of the breastbone. Then cut through the backbone to split the bird in half. If liked, cut along the backbone and remove, this may then be used in the stock pot and means that you serve less bone on the plate. Cut each half in two making a slanting cut between the ribs to separate the wing and the leg; this will make 4 good portions.

CASSEROLES

The choice is yours. It ranges from breast of lamb for an inexpensive and
filling family meal to steak with cream and horseradish for a dinner party.
It takes in good British beef and dumplings, Italian osso buco made with
knuckle of veal, chilli con carne from Mexico, and of course Irish stew. You
can use chicken, pork, game and all the vegetables you want.

The casserole is the cook's most versatile dish. It can hardly be cooked
too long. It can be prepared well in advance and allowed to cook slowly
until needed, and it can remain without spoiling in the oven for
latecomers. Long, slow cooking makes tough meat tender, so that cheaper
kinds can be used, while it enhances the flavour of the more expensive cuts.

Casserole meals are easy to serve as the vegetables are cooked along
with the meat, adding their own distinction to the seasonings, herbs and
spices that make up the delicious whole.

Carbonnade of beef   *Serves 4*

There is no stock in this recipe, just beer, so that the result is full of flavour.

675 g (1½ lb) shin of beef
40 g (1½ oz) dripping
350 g (12 oz) onions, sliced
75 g (3 oz) chopped bacon
40 g (1½ oz) flour

450 ml (15 fl oz) pale ale
1½ tsp salt
Ground black pepper
A little gravy browning
2 tbsp chopped parsley to garnish

Cut the meat into 1·25 cm (½ in) thick strips.

Melt the dripping in a pan and quickly brown the meat, lift out with a
slotted spoon and place on one side. Add the onions and bacon to the pan
and fry quickly until golden brown. Stir in the flour and cook for a minute,
then gradually blend in the ale and bring to the boil, stirring until
thickened. Add the salt, pepper and a little gravy browning and return the
meat to the pan. Cover and simmer gently for 3–4 hours or until the meat
is tender.

Taste and check seasoning. Turn into a warm serving dish and sprinkle
with parsley and serve.

Veal and tomato casserole   *Serves 4*

A lovely way of serving pie veal, full of flavour.

1 tbsp oil
25 g (1 oz) butter
675 g (1½ lb) pie veal
1 large onion, chopped
25 g (1 oz) flour
150 ml (5 fl oz) dry white wine or cider

150 ml (5 fl oz) chicken stock
225 g (8 oz) can peeled tomatoes
Salt and pepper
100 g (4 oz) button mushrooms, sliced
A little chopped parsley mixed with
 finely grated lemon rind to garnish

Heat the oil and butter in a saucepan and fry the veal and onion for 3–4 minutes. Stir in the flour and cook for a minute. Blend in the wine and stock and bring to the boil. Add the tomatoes and season well. Cover the pan and simmer for 1½ hours, add the mushrooms and continue cooking for a further 15 minutes or until the veal is tender.

Taste and check seasoning and then turn into a warm casserole or serving dish. Sprinkle the top with the parsley and lemon mixture.

Casseroled meat balls   Serves 4

A very good way of using up small tomatoes at the end of the summer. This dish is a meal in itself and is ideal to leave in the oven for the family.

450 g (1 lb) minced beef
50 g (2 oz) fresh white breadcrumbs
2 tsp Worcestershire sauce
1 level tsp salt
Freshly ground black pepper
1 egg, beaten
25 g (1 oz) flour
2 tbsp oil
1 large onion, sliced

225 g (8 oz) carrots, diced
450 g (1 lb) small potatoes, quartered
  lengthwise
350 g (12 oz) small whole tomatoes,
  peeled
¼ level tsp dried sage
1 bay leaf
600 ml (1 pt) beef stock

Heat the oven to 180° C (350° F), gas mark 4.

Put the minced beef, breadcrumbs, Worcestershire sauce, seasoning and egg in a bowl and mix thoroughly, then form into 16 small balls and coat in the flour.

Heat the oil in a frying pan and fry the meat balls and onion until brown, then lift out with a slotted spoon and place in a large casserole with the carrots, potatoes, tomatoes, sage and bay leaf.

Add any remaining flour to the pan and cook for a minute, stir in the stock and bring to the boil, stirring, and simmer for 2 minutes. Season and then pour into the casserole, cover and bake in the oven for about 1½ hours or until all the vegetables are tender. Remove the bay leaf before serving.

French beef in red wine   Serves 6

Not a cheap dish to make but really worthwhile. It also freezes well.

6 slices topside of beef
175 g (6 oz) streaky bacon
25 g (1 oz) bacon fat or dripping
12·5 g (½ oz) flour
300 ml (10 fl oz) beef stock
150 ml (5 fl oz) cheap red wine
1 bay leaf

½ tsp chopped fresh herbs
A sprig of parsley
½ tsp salt
Freshly ground black pepper
12 small white onions
175 g (6 oz) button mushrooms

Lamb kebabs (page 81)

Heat the oven to 160° C (325° F), gas mark 3.

Trim any excess fat from the meat if necessary. De-rind and chop the bacon. Melt the fat or dripping in a large pan and fry the bacon in it until it is crisp. Remove with a slotted spoon and put in a 1·7 l (3 pt) ovenproof casserole. Fry the beef in the fat remaining in the pan until brown on both sides and lift out and add to the casserole.

Blend in the flour and cook until browned, then stir in the stock, wine and herbs and bring to the boil, stirring until thickened; season well. Pour it over the meat, cover and cook in the oven for 1½ hours.

Peel the onions and leave whole, add to the casserole with the mushrooms and cook for a further hour or until the meat is tender.

Taste and check seasoning and remove the bay leaf before serving. If necessary skim off any excess fat.

To freeze: cool, turn into a container, cover and label. When required, leave to thaw overnight in the refrigerator and then reheat in the oven at 190° C (375° F), gas mark 5 for 45 minutes or until piping hot.

Beef Marseilles   *Serves 4–6*

A very tasty beef stew, typical of the south of France, that is so easy to prepare. A long, slow cooking is essential to get the full flavour.

675 g (1½ lb) chuck steak
300 ml (10 fl oz) red wine
2 tsbp oil
Ground black pepper
1 bay leaf
1–2 cloves garlic, crushed
1 large onion, sliced
4 carrots, sliced

175 g (6 oz) unsmoked streaky bacon
350 g (12 oz) tomatoes, peeled,
  quartered and seeded
Salt

100 g (4 oz) mushrooms,
  sliced
8 black olives, stoned and sliced

Cut the meat into 5 cm (2 in) squares and put into a china bowl with the wine, oil, pepper, bay leaf and garlic. Then add the onion and carrots and stir well, cover and leave in a cool place to marinade for at least 4 hours or preferably overnight.

Next day heat the oven to 150° C (300° F), gas mark 2.

Cut the bacon into strips, removing any rind and bone and place half in the base of a 1·7 l (3 pt) casserole, put the meat on top with the vegetables and marinade and then add the remaining bacon and tomatoes. Season with salt, cover and cook in the oven for 3½ hours or longer until the meat is tender.

Add the mushrooms and olives for the last 30 minutes of the cooking time. Check seasoning, remove the bay leaf and serve with creamed potatoes.

Braised oxtail and Spanish tuna pie (pages 53 and 105)

Chilli con carne   *Serves 6*

If you like a very potent Chilli add a little more powder, but take care – it is easy to make it too hot. Chilli powder varies considerably in spiciness among different brands, so check carefully before adding too much (I have used McCormack for this recipe).

100 g (4 oz) streaky bacon
2 onions, chopped
675 g (1½ lb) minced beef
2 cloves garlic, crushed
25 g (1 oz) flour
1 level tsp chilli powder

450 ml (15 fl oz) water
70 g (2¼ oz) can tomato purée
2 sticks celery, chopped
Salt and pepper
396 g (14 oz) can kidney beans, drained

Remove the rind and bone from the bacon and cut into strips and put in a pan with the onion, beef and garlic and fry gently for about 5 minutes to let the fat run out, stirring frequently.

Stir in the flour and chilli powder and cook for a minute. Add the water and tomato purée and stir well, add the celery and season well, bring to the boil and then cover the pan, reduce the heat and simmer for 45 minutes.

Add the kidney beans and simmer for a further 15 minutes. Taste and check seasoning and serve with plain boiled rice and a green salad.

Irish stew   *Serves 4*

Not quite authentic! True Irish stew is just lamb and potatoes but I think carrots go well too. If you dislike too many bones in the stew make it with neck fillet of lamb which can be boned out from the scrag end of neck in one piece. Cut into 2·5 cm (1 in) chunks and make the stew in the same way. Allow 450 g (1 lb) meat for 4 people.

1·1 kg (2½ lb) middle neck of lamb
2 large onions
225 g (8 oz) carrots (optional)

450 g (1 lb) potatoes
Salt and pepper
Chopped parsley to garnish

Heat the oven to 160° C (325° F), gas mark 3.

Cut the lamb in neat pieces and remove the spinal cord. Peel and slice the onions and carrots and potatoes. Alternate layers of meat with layers of each vegetable in a 1·7 l (3 pt) ovenproof casserole, seasoning each layer with salt and pepper and finishing with a layer of potato.

Pour in just sufficient water to come halfway up the casserole. Cover with a lid and cook in the oven for 2½ hours or until the meat is nearly tender. Remove the lid, increase the heat in the oven to 180° C (350° F), gas mark 4 and cook for a further 30 minutes or until the top layer of potato is brown. Garnish with chopped parsley.

Osso buco *Serves 4*

A very rich Italian stew which is traditionally made from knuckle of veal with the marrow in the bone carefully preserved in its entirety. If you have difficulty in getting knuckle, make this dish with shin or pie veal instead. This dish freezes well, too.

900 g–1·1 kg (2–2½ lb) knuckle veal or
  675 g (1½ lb) pie veal
1 tbsp oil
12·5 g (½ oz) butter
3 carrots, sliced
2 sticks celery, chopped
1 onion, chopped
1 clove garlic, crushed
1 tbsp flour

150 ml (5 fl oz) dry white wine
300 ml (10 fl oz) chicken stock
397 g (14 oz) can tomatoes
A sprig of parsley
1 bay leaf
Salt and pepper
Grated rind of half a lemon mixed with
  2 tbsp chopped parsley to garnish

Heat the oven to 160° C (325° F), gas mark 3.

Ask your butcher to saw the knuckle into 5 cm (2 in) sized chunks or, if using pie veal, cut into 3·5 cm (1½ in) pieces. Heat the oil in a large frying pan, add the butter and fry half the meat at a time until golden brown. Take care not to let the marrow slip out of the knuckle bone. Drain on kitchen paper then transfer to a 1·7 l (3 pt) casserole.

Fry the vegetables in the fat remaining in the pan for 5 minutes. Stir in the flour and cook until browned, then add the remaining ingredients except the garnish. Bring to the boil and pour over the meat. Cover the casserole and cook in the oven for about 3 hours. Taste and check seasoning, sprinkle with the garnish and serve.

To freeze: cool, turn into a rigid container. Cover, label and freeze. To serve: turn into an ovenproof casserole, cover and reheat in a moderate oven 180° C (350° F), gas mark 4 for 40–60 minutes until hot through, stirring occasionally. Sprinkle with the garnish and serve.

Beef and orange casserole *Serves 4–6*

An unusual recipe well worth trying, it makes an inexpensive and easy dish for entertaining.

675 g (1½ lb) chuck steak
225 g (8 oz) onions
225 g (8 oz) carrots
25 g (1 oz) dripping
Salt
900 ml (1½ pt) packet oxtail soup
600 ml (1 pt) water

1 orange
8 cloves

Cut the steak into 2·5 cm (1 in) cubes and slice the onions and carrots. Melt the dripping in a saucepan and fry the onion and meat for 3–4 minutes. Stir in the carrots and salt and then add the contents of the soup packet and the water and bring to the boil, stirring until thickened.

Cut the orange in half and stick 4 cloves into the skin of each half, add to the pan, cover and simmer until the meat is tender – about 2½ hours. Lift out the oranges with a spoon and fork and squeeze any juice back into the pan, discard the skins.

Taste and check seasoning and serve with creamed potatoes and a green vegetable.

Argyll lamb   *Serves 4*

Breasts of lamb are inexpensive and if cooked in this way they make a delicious main meal. Serve with chunky tomato sauce.

2 breasts of lamb	*1 tbsp vinegar*
Salt and pepper	*50 g (2 oz) butter*
1 carrot	*450 g (1 lb) onions, sliced*
1 onion	*50 g (2 oz) fresh white breadcrumbs*
1 bay leaf	*50 g (2 oz) Cheddar cheese, grated*
A sprig of parsley	

Put the meat in a saucepan with the seasoning, carrot, onion, bay leaf, parsley and vinegar and add just sufficient water to cover the meat. Bring to the boil and then cover the pan and simmer gently for 1–1½ hours or until the meat is quite tender and the bones will easily pull out. Lift out the meat and remove all the bones and any excess fat, cut the meat into neat serving strips and arrange in a shallow ovenproof dish.

Melt the butter in a saucepan and fry the onions gently for 10–15 minutes or until they are soft and then spoon over the meat. Mix the breadcrumbs and cheese together and sprinkle over the onions.

When required bake in the oven at 190° C (375° F), gas mark 5 for 25 minutes until the top is a pale golden brown and crisp. Serve with a good tomato sauce.

Spiced pork   *Serves 4–6*

Serve with creamy mashed potato to sop up the gravy.

675 g (1½ lb) stewing pork	*397 g (14 oz) can peeled tomatoes*
25 g (1 oz) dripping	*150 ml (5 fl oz) stock*
225 g (8 oz) onions, sliced	*1 rounded tbsp chutney*
1 clove garlic, crushed	*1 rounded tbsp apricot jam or honey*

25 g (1 oz) flour   *Salt and pepper*
1 level tbsp made mustard

Cut the pork into 2·5 cm (1 in) cubes. Melt the dripping in the pan and fry the pork with the onions and garlic until lightly browned. Stir in the flour and cook for a minute, then add the remaining ingredients and season well.

   Cover the pan and simmer gently for 1½–2 hours or until tender.

Braised oxtail   *Serves 6 (See colour plate facing page 49)*

A great favourite. Take care to skim off every scrap of fat once the oxtail is cooked. It takes at least 4 hours to cook and must be simmered very gently for the best results.

1·3 kg (3 lb) oxtail in pieces   *2 bay leaves*
50 g (2 oz) lard or dripping   *3 sprigs parsley*
2 onions, chopped   *6 peppercorns*
2 large carrots, chopped   *Salt*
½ head celery, chopped   *1·1 l (2 pt) water*
2 rashers streaky bacon, chopped   *2 beef stock cubes*
25 g (1 oz) flour   *Gravy browning*

Trim off any excess fat from the oxtail joints. Heat the lard or dripping in a pan, add the oxtail and brown quickly on all sides, then remove from the pan and put on one side. Add the vegetables and bacon to the pan, cook gently for 5 minutes. Blend in the flour, cook for one minute, then blend in the remaining ingredients except the browning and bring to the boil, stirring until thickened slightly. Return the oxtail to the pan, cover and simmer for about 4 hours or until the meat can be easily removed from the bones.

   Place on a serving dish and keep hot, with the vegetables arranged around. Boil the sauce rapidly until reduced to 450 ml (15 fl oz), remove the parsley and bay leaf, check seasoning, add a little gravy browning, then strain over the oxtail.

Goulash   *Serves 4–6*

A colourful casserole that is nice served with buttered noodles or plain boiled rice.

675 g (1½ lb) stewing steak   *397 g (14 oz) can peeled tomatoes*
25 g (1 oz) dripping   *300 ml (10 fl oz) stock*
225 g (8 oz) onions, sliced   *Salt and pepper*
2 level tbsp paprika   *2 potatoes, peeled and diced*
25 g (1 oz) flour

Cut the meat into neat pieces. Melt the dripping in a saucepan and fry the meat for 3–4 minutes to quickly seal and brown, then lift out with a slotted spoon and put on one side. Add the onions to the pan and fry for 5 minutes to lightly brown. Stir in the paprika and flour and cook for one minute, then add the tomatoes, stock and seasoning and bring to the boil, stirring until thickened. Return the meat to the pan, partially cover and simmer for 1½ hours and then add the potatoes and continue cooking for a further hour or until the meat is tender.

Taste and check seasoning and serve very hot with buttered noodles.

Bacon hot pot   *Serves 6–8*

A good filling winter dish; no need to serve any extra vegetables, just a few simply cooked potatoes.

675 g (1½ lb) collar of bacon	*4 sticks celery, cut in thick slices*
175 g (6 oz) butter beans	*300 ml (10 fl oz) stock*
12 button onions	*227 g (8 oz) packet frozen mixed vegetables*

Soak the bacon overnight. Place the butter beans in a small bowl and cover with cold water and leave to soak with the bacon overnight.

Heat the oven to 190° C (375° F), gas mark 5.

Drain the water from the bacon and butter beans and put them in a large ovenproof casserole with the onions, celery and stock. Cover and cook in the oven for an hour. Then remove the lid and stir in the mixed vegetables. Return to the oven and continue cooking for a further 15 minutes or until everything is tender.

Buckingham beef   *Serves 8*

This is unusual, quite sweet and spiced; the walnuts should be added at the end of the cooking time so that they are still crunchy when the dish is served.

100 g (4 oz) dried apricots	*1 tbsp soy sauce*
600 ml (1 pt) dry cider	*2 cloves garlic, crushed*
1·1 kg (2½ lb) leg of beef	*100 g (4 oz) seedless raisins*
4 tbsp oil	*25 g (1 oz) dark soft brown sugar*
225 g (8 oz) onions, chopped	*A sprig of fresh thyme*
50 g (2 oz) flour	*Salt and ground black pepper*
150–300 ml (5–10 fl oz) beef stock	*75 g (3 oz) walnuts, coarsely chopped*
Juice of 2 oranges	*Chopped parsley to garnish*
1 level tsp curry powder	

Soak the apricots in the cider overnight. Heat the oven to 160° C (325° F), gas mark 3 on the day.

Cut the beef into 1·25 cm (½ in) cubes. Heat the oil in a large pan and fry the meat until browned all over. Lift out with a slotted spoon and put in a large casserole, add the onions to the oil remaining in the pan and fry until lightly browned. Sprinkle over the flour and allow to brown, add the cider and apricots and bring to the boil, stirring until thickened. Add 150 ml (5 fl oz) stock, orange juice, curry powder, soy sauce, garlic, raisins, sugar, thyme and seasoning. Pour over the meat, cover and cook in the oven for 2–2½ hours or until the meat is tender. Stir in the walnuts for the last 15 minutes of the cooking time.

Taste and check seasoning and remove the sprig of thyme. If the gravy is too thick add a little extra stock. Sprinkle with chopped parsley and serve.

Boiled salt silverside with mustard sauce   *Serves 8*

You might well think that mustard sauce does not go with boiled beef but it does. As a child it was a great favourite with boiled onions and carrots topped with chopped parsley.

Order the silverside at least a week in advance, you will need to get it from an old fashioned sort of family butcher as it is not usually found in supermarkets. Some butchers only keep the brine used for salting available in colder weather. Take care to simmer slowly otherwise the meat will shrink.

1·3 kg (3 lb) piece salt silverside or boned and rolled salt brisket of beef	*225 g (8 oz) small carrots* *225 g (8 oz) small onions*

Sauce
50 g (2 oz) butter
50 g (2 oz) flour
300 ml (10 fl oz) milk
1 level tbsp dry mustard

1 level tbsp brown sugar
3 tbsp vinegar
Salt and pepper

Wash the meat in cold water and if necessary soak overnight to remove any excess salt.

Place in a large saucepan, cover with cold water and bring to the boil. Peel the carrots and onions and leave whole. Cover the pan with a lid and simmer very gently, allowing 35 minutes for each 450 g (1 lb) and 35 minutes over. Add the vegetables to the pan for the last hour of the cooking time. Lift the meat out onto a serving dish and place the vegetables around and keep warm.

Then make the sauce. Melt the butter in a pan, add the flour and cook for 2 minutes. Stir in the milk and 300 ml (10 fl oz) of the cooking liquor, bring to the boil and simmer for 2 minutes to thicken the sauce. Blend the mustard with the sugar and vinegar and stir into the sauce and mix well, season to taste and serve with the meat.

Navarin of lamb   *Serves 4 (See colour plate facing page 72)*

This stew is full of vegetables and is a meal on its own but for those who are very hungry serve chunks of French bread.

900 g–1 kg (2–2½ lb) middle neck of lamb cut in pieces	*1 onion, chopped*
25 g (1 oz) seasoned flour	*225 g (8 oz) young carrots, sliced*
50 g (2 oz) dripping	*2 small turnips, peeled and diced*
600 ml (1 pt) stock	*Salt and pepper*
2 level tbsp tomato purée	*12 small new potatoes*
	100 g (4 oz) peas

Heat the oven to 160° C (325° F), gas mark 3.

Trim any excess fat from the lamb and coat in seasoned flour. Melt the dripping in a large frying pan and fry the meat quickly to brown on both sides. Lift out and place in a large 2·5 l (4½ pt) ovenproof casserole.

Stir any remaining flour into the fat in the pan and cook for 2 minutes. Add the stock and tomato purée and bring to the boil, stirring until slightly thickened.

Add the onion, carrots and turnips to the casserole and then pour over the hot stock, season well, cover with a tight fitting lid and cook in the oven for 1 hour.

Add the potatoes to the casserole, making sure that they are pushed down into the gravy and continue cooking for a further 30 minutes, then stir in the peas and cook for 15 minutes.

Taste and check seasoning and serve at once.

Beef cobbler   *Serves 4–6*

This recipe is also almost a meal in itself – just serve a green vegetable, such as cabbage or sprouts. A filling winter dish.

25 g (1 oz) dripping	*1 bay leaf*
675 g (1½ lb) stewing steak	*4 medium potatoes, peeled and halved*
25 g (1 oz) flour	*225 g (8 oz) carrots, peeled and quartered*
600 ml (1 pt) beef stock	*2 large leeks, sliced*
Salt and pepper	

Cobbler topping
175 g (6 oz) self-raising flour	*Pinch mixed dried herbs*
75 g (3 oz) margarine	*6–7 tbsp milk*
½ level tsp salt	

Heat the oven to 160° C (325° F), gas mark 3.

Melt the dripping in a frying pan, cut the meat into 2·5 cm (1 in) cubes and add to the pan and quickly fry to seal the juices. Add the flour and cook for a minute until lightly browned, blend in the stock and bring to the boil, stirring until the sauce has thickened slightly. Add the seasoning and bay leaf and turn into a large casserole about 2·3 l (4 pt). Cover and cook in the oven for 1½ hours and then add the vegetables and continue cooking for a further hour.

Turn the oven up to 190° C (375° F), gas mark 5.

Prepare the topping: put the flour in a bowl, add the margarine and rub in with the fingertips until the mixture resembles fine breadcrumbs, add the salt and herbs and stir in the milk to make a soft but not sticky dough. Turn onto a lightly floured table and knead lightly and roll out to 1·8 cm (¾ in) thickness and cut into 8–10 rounds of 5 cm (2 in) each.

Remove the lid from the casserole and lift out the bay leaf. Arrange the cobbler on top, brush with a little milk and then return, uncovered, to the oven for about 20 minutes or until well risen and golden brown.

Serve at once with a green vegetable.

Swiss steak   *Serves 4*

A good meaty casserole just right for a cold night.

4 slices topside of beef, each weighing about 175 g (6 oz)	*2 large onions, finely sliced*
40 g (1½ oz) flour	*2 sticks celery, sliced*
1 level tsp salt	*227 g (8 oz) can peeled tomatoes*
¼ level tsp pepper	*2 level tsp tomato purée*
40 g (1½ oz) lard or dripping	*1 tsp Worcestershire sauce*
	150 ml (5 fl oz) stock

Heat the oven to 150° C (300° F), gas mark 2.

Cut the beef into 8 pieces. Mix together the flour, salt and pepper; toss the meat in the flour mixture pressing it so that most of the flour is used.

Melt the lard or dripping in a pan and fry the meat quickly on all sides until it is browned, lift out and transfer to an ovenproof casserole.

Add the onion and celery to the fat remaining in the pan and fry until a pale golden brown and then add to the meat in the casserole; if there should be any flour left over stir it into the vegetables and cook for a minute. Add the tomatoes, purée, Worcestershire sauce and stock to the casserole.

Cover and cook in the oven for about 2½ hours or until the meat is tender.

Sweet spiced pork curry   *Serves 6*

As a variation make this with chicken instead; the cooking time will be slightly shorter.

900 g (2 lb) lean pork
40 g (1½ oz) flour
1½ tsp salt
1 large onion, peeled and chopped
50 g (2 oz) margarine
1 level tbsp hot curry powder or flavour
  to taste

1 level tbsp paprika pepper
300 ml (10 fl oz) stock
2 dried red chillies
1 tbsp mango chutney
1 tsp Worcestershire sauce
450 g (1 lb) can pineapple cubes
2 bay leaves

Cut the pork into 2 cm (¾ in) cubes and toss in the flour and salt. Put the onion in a saucepan with the margarine and fry until soft, stir in the curry powder and paprika and fry for 5 minutes, then add the pork and stir well and fry for another 5 minutes.

Add all the remaining ingredients to the pan including the pineapple syrup, cover and cook gently for 1½–2 hours or until the pork is tender. If preferred the curry may be turned into an ovenproof dish and cooked in the oven at 160° C (325° F), gas mark 3 for about the same time. A long, slow cook is always best for a curry as it brings out the flavour.

Remove the bay leaves and chillies, taste and check seasoning and serve with boiled rice.

Beef olives   *Serves 4*

An unusual way of serving beef with a gorgeous flavour.

4 slices topside of beef 1·8 cm (¾ in)
  thick
4 tsp horseradish cream
Salt and pepper
2 small carrots, scraped and cut into
  strips

1 small onion, finely chopped
1 celery stalk, cut into strips
19 g (¾ oz) flour
2 tbsp oil
450 ml (15 fl oz) tomato juice
5 tbsp red wine

Remove any fat from the meat and place the slices between two sheets of dampened greaseproof paper and beat with a rolling pin until they are very thin. Remove the paper, spread each slice of meat with a spoonful of horseradish cream and season well. Lay the vegetables on top and roll up the meat slices. Secure with thin string and then coat each roll in the flour.

Heat the oil in a pan and add the rolls and quickly fry until brown all round. Add the tomato juice and wine, cover the pan and simmer very gently for about 1¾ hours or until tender.

Remove the string before serving with noodles.

Beef and vegetable stew with dumplings   *Serves 4 (See cover photograph)*

A traditional stew full of flavour, made with plenty of root vegetables and served with fluffy parsley dumplings.

675 g (1½ lb) stewing steak
25 g (1 oz) flour
25 g (1 oz) dripping
2 carrots, sliced
2 onions, sliced

1 parsnip, diced
1 small turnip, diced
450 ml (15 fl oz) beef stock
Salt and pepper
1 bay leaf

Dumplings
100 g (4 oz) self-raising flour
50 g (2 oz) prepared suet
½ level tsp salt

1 level tbsp fresh chopped parsley
About 5–6 tbsp water

Cut the beef into 2·5 cm (1 in) cubes and coat in flour. Melt the dripping in a pan and fry the meat and vegetables for about 4 minutes. Stir in any remaining flour, add the stock and bring to the boil, stirring, season well and add the bay leaf. Cover and simmer for 1½–2 hours or until the beef is nearly tender. Then remove the bay leaf and taste and check seasoning.

Now prepare the dumplings. Put the flour in a bowl with the suet, salt and herbs, add water and mix to a soft, but not sticky, dough and form into 8 balls, drop on top of the stew, cover the pan and simmer for 30 minutes until well risen and fluffy. Serve the stew at once.

Manor house beef   *Serves 4–6*

A light casserole with an unusual garnish with lots of crunch.

675 g (1½ lb) chuck steak
25 g (1 oz) dripping
2 onions, thinly sliced
4 sticks celery, sliced
25 g (1 oz) flour
150 ml (5 fl oz) red wine

450 ml (15 fl oz) beef stock
1 bay leaf
Salt
Ground black pepper
25 g (1 oz) walnut halves to garnish

Heat the oven to 160° C (325° F), gas mark 3.

Cut the meat into 2·5 cm (1 in) cubes. Heat the dripping in a frying pan and fry the meat for 4–5 minutes until browned and then lift out with a slotted spoon and place in an ovenproof casserole. Add the onions and celery to the pan and fry quickly for 2 minutes. Stir in the flour and cook for 2 minutes, blend in the wine and the stock and bring to the boil, stirring until thickened, add the bay leaf and season well and then pour over the meat. Cover and cook in the oven for 1½–2 hours or until the meat is tender.

Remove the bay leaf, check seasoning and sprinkle with the walnuts.

Red pork   *Serves 4–6*

A really different casserole with a superb flavour; all that is needed to make it a complete meal is some potatoes, simply cooked.

450 g (1 lb) pie pork
12·5 g (½ oz) seasoned flour
25 g (1 oz) dripping
2 large onions, chopped
450 g (1 lb) red cabbage, shredded
225 g (8 oz) cooking apples, weighed
 after peeling and coring

150 ml (5 fl oz) water
1 tsp salt
4 cloves
2 tbsp vinegar
1 rounded tbsp redcurrant
 jelly

Cut the pork into 1·25 cm (½ in) pieces and coat each in the flour. Melt the dripping in a pan and fry the pork and onions for 5 minutes.

Trim, clean and finely shred the cabbage, slice the apples and add both to the pan with the water, salt and cloves, stir thoroughly and then cover with a tight fitting lid and simmer gently for 1½ hours or until the pork is tender.

Remove the cloves and add the vinegar and redcurrant jelly, stir lightly so that the jelly melts. Taste and check seasoning and then serve piping hot.

Braised beef in red wine   *Serves 4 (See colour plate facing page 73)*

A long, slow cooking helps the flavour of the wine be absorbed into the meat.

4 portions chuck steak, each about
 175 g (6 oz)
A little seasoned flour
25 g (1 oz) dripping
2 large onions, chopped

3 large carrots, sliced
1 parsnip or turnip, peeled and diced
300 ml (10 fl oz) red wine
Salt and pepper
1 bay leaf

Heat the oven to 150° C (300° F), gas mark 2.

Lightly coat the meat in seasoned flour. Melt the dripping in a frying pan and quickly fry the meat to brown on both sides, lift out and put on one side. Add the vegetables to the fat remaining in the pan and fry for 2–3 minutes then lift out and put in an ovenproof casserole, lay the meat on top.

Add the wine to the pan and bring to the boil, then pour over the meat and vegetables and season well, add the bay leaf. Cover the casserole with a tight fitting lid and then cook in the oven for about 2½ hours or until the meat and vegetables are tender.

Remove the bay leaf, taste and adjust seasoning. Serve very hot with creamed potatoes.

DINNER PARTIES

Dinner parties are special. Your guests deserve your full attention and the food deserves thought, planning and preparation, in cooking and in presentation. The setting will be right, the drinks will be right – so will the conversation. And so, above all, will be the food.

Dinner party menus must be built round the main course, the centrepiece of the meal that dictates the first course, the sweet and the wine. Here are some main dishes that can carry any dinner party. They have been tried and tested and come up smiling every time.

Seek out special ingredients and take all the trouble you can over the preparations. You are not economising on time or money – this is an occasion. If you can, for instance, find a shop selling poussins, or if you spend time on a special sauce for pork, or take time to make colourful garnishes, then you are going to earn yourself a well deserved reputation as a hostess.

And if you do your work well ahead, so that you have time for your guests, and if you provide dishes that are easy to serve at table, then everyone will be pleased.

Chicken peri peri   *Serves 6*

A very spicy way of cooking chicken that goes well with rice or buttered noodles; then all that is needed is a green salad.

2 tbsp oil	70 g (2½ oz) can tomato purée
350 g (12 oz) onions, chopped	6 peppercorns
350 g (12 oz) tomatoes, skinned and	1 clove
sliced	1 tbsp vinegar
½ level tsp chilli powder	Salt and pepper
1 clove garlic	600 ml (1 pt) water
1 level tsp curry powder	6 chicken portions
1 bay leaf	150 ml (5 fl oz) soured cream

Heat the oil in a pan and add the onions and fry for about 5 minutes and then add all the other ingredients except the chicken and cream. Bring to the boil, partially cover and simmer for 30 minutes.

Skin the chicken and lay in an ovenproof casserole.

Heat the oven to 150° C (300° F), gas mark 2.

Carefully lift the bay leaf, peppercorns and clove from the sauce and then purée in a blender in 2 or 3 batches until quite smooth, pour over the chicken, cover and cook in the oven for about 1½ hours or until the chicken is very tender. Cool and then leave overnight in the refrigerator.

Next day reheat in a hot oven, 200° C (400° F), gas mark 6, for 40 minutes or until chicken and sauce are piping hot.

As you serve the chicken stir a spoonful of cream into each portion so that it has an attractive swirled effect.

Poussins farcis   *Serves 2*

Poussins are specially bred baby chickens and really different. Serve one per person. They are difficult to come by in smaller butchers, but specialist butchers have them, although they may need to be ordered; you may also be lucky in some large supermarkets and freezer centres. I ate them cooked this way in Seville at a very grand dinner; they were superb and perfect for an anniversary or special dinner for two at home.

2 poussins

Stuffing
25 g (1 oz) butter
1 small onion, chopped
12·5 g (½ oz) chopped almonds
1 rounded tbsp chopped watercress

50 g (2 oz) fresh white breadcrumbs
Salt and pepper
A little beaten egg

Sauce
1 level tbsp flour
150 ml (5 fl oz) stock

2–3 tbsp port

Wipe out the poussins and season well inside. Heat the oven to 190° C (375° F), gas mark 5.

Melt the butter in a pan and add the onion and fry for about 5 minutes, then stir in the almonds and fry for 2–3 minutes until pale golden brown, stir in the watercress, breadcrumbs and seasoning and then add just sufficient beaten egg to bind and stuff into the neck end of the poussins. Dot the breast of the birds with butter, put in a baking tin and cover them with a piece of greaseproof paper or foil and roast in the oven for 30 minutes, then remove the paper or foil and continue cooking for a further 15 minutes or until golden brown and tender.

Lift out the poussins and place on a warm serving dish. Stir the flour into the juices in the pan and cook over a moderate heat for 2 minutes, then stir in the stock and port and bring to the boil, stirring until thickened, taste and check seasoning and serve with the poussins.

Serve with broccoli and straw potatoes made by cutting potatoes into strips like matchsticks and deep frying until golden brown.

Chicken parcels   *Serves 8*

The special sort of dish that is perfect for entertaining – no carving or portioning to do at table – and it may be prepared the day ahead or early in the morning. Each chicken breast is wrapped in slices of ham with a little mushroom sauce and then in puff pastry. If the chicken breasts are very large you could cut them in half or use boneless chicken meat bought from the freezer centre and then thawed; for eight people you would need 900 g (2 lb) of chicken meat.

8 small boneless chicken breasts or 4
  large halved
62·5 g (2½ oz) butter
2 tbsp oil
About 2 tbsp seasoned flour

Sauce
62·5 g (2½ oz) butter
50 g (2 oz) flour
450 ml (15 fl oz) stock saved from the
  chicken breasts
150 ml (5 fl oz) dry sherry

450 ml (15 fl oz) chicken stock
¼ tsp nutmeg
Salt and pepper
350 g (12 oz) white button mushrooms,
  thinly sliced

150 ml (5 fl oz) single cream
2 blocks, 397 g (14 oz) each, frozen puff
  pastry, thawed
Beaten egg to glaze
8 slices ham

Carefully remove any bones and skin from the chicken. Melt 25 g (1 oz) butter in a large, shallow pan, add the oil. Toss the chicken in seasoned flour and add to the pan and brown on all sides, lift out into a saucepan and cover with stock, nutmeg and seasoning. Bring to the boil, cover with a lid and simmer gently for about 20 minutes or until tender. Strain off the stock and put the chicken on one side.

Next fry the mushrooms in a shallow pan in the remaining butter for 3 minutes, season and turn onto a plate with any juices. Rinse out the pan and use to make the sauce; melt the butter, add the flour and cook gently until a pale golden colour, add the reserved stock little by little, adding all but about 70 ml (2½ fl oz) and blend well until smooth. Add the sherry and the juices from the mushrooms, and bring to the boil, stirring until thickened and simmer for 2 minutes, taste and check seasoning. Pour half of this sauce into a bowl and leave to cool.

Add the reserved stock to the sauce in the pan and stir in until blended; this sauce may then be put in a container and covered and left in the refrigerator until ready to reheat and serve as a sauce for the chicken.

Roll out both blocks of pastry to 32·5 cm (13 in) squares and divide each into 4 squares and brush the edges with a little beaten egg. Lay 8 slices of ham flat on the table and place a spoonful of mushrooms and some sauce on each with a breast of chicken and roll up each slice of ham. Place a ham roll in the centre of each square of pastry and fold the pastry over. Seal the edges carefully pressing well together, decorate with leaves cut from the pastry trimmings, fix in place with a little beaten egg. Chill in the refrigerator until required.

Heat the oven to 220° C (425° F), gas mark 7.

Put the parcels on a baking tray and glaze with beaten egg. Bake for 30 minutes or until the pastry is well risen and golden brown. Reheat the sauce until boiling, remove from the heat and add the single cream, keep hot but do not re-boil, check seasoning and serve in a sauceboat with the chicken parcels. Only one vegetable need be served, such as broccoli spears which go well with the sauce.

Fantastic chicken   *Serves 12*

A lovely bright saffron yellow sauce. Serve for celebrations; it is just right for a buffet supper. Make the sauce a couple of days ahead then mix with the chicken a day ahead and put in the refrigerator for the flavours to blend. Add the grapes just before serving.

Use turkey for larger quantities or on New Year's Eve, a 2·7 kg (6 lb) capon or chicken should give you enough meat for 12. Serve with assorted salads and French bread.

1 tbsp oil	*900 g (2 lb) cooked chopped turkey or*
1 onion, chopped	*chicken*
2 tbsp tomato purée	*225 g (8 oz) green and black grapes,*
4 tbsp lemon juice	*halved and stoned*
4 tbsp apricot jam	*Salt*
1 level tsp curry powder	*Ground black pepper*
¼ tsp turmeric	*40 g (1½ oz) browned flaked almonds*
450 ml (15 fl oz) good mayonnaise	*Small sprigs watercress or parsley to*
	garnish

Put the oil and onion in a small saucepan and fry for about 5 minutes or until the onion is tender but not brown, then add the tomato purée, 2 tbsp lemon juice, apricot jam, curry powder and turmeric, bring to the boil, stirring and simmer for 5 minutes, cool slightly and then purée in a blender. When quite cold blend with the mayonnaise, stir in the chicken, taste and season if necessary, chill overnight in the refrigerator.

Toss the grapes in the remaining lemon juice and stir into the mayonnaise. Pile into a serving dish and sprinkle with the browned flaked almonds. Garnish the dish with small sprigs of watercress or parsley.

French lamb roast   *Serves 10–12*

Roast leg of lamb is not one of the easiest to carve. In this recipe the lamb is carved in advance and a rich mushroom stuffing slotted in between the slices of meat; the joint is then put back in the oven to finish roasting. It takes time and care, so do it before your guests arrive.

1 small leg of lamb	*25 g (1 oz) butter*
Garlic	*300 ml (10 fl oz) dry cider*
Stuffing	
225 g (8 oz) mushrooms	*1 level tbsp fresh chopped mixed herbs*
25 g (1 oz) butter	*75 g (3 oz) fresh white breadcrumbs*
1 small onion, finely chopped	*Salt and pepper*
Topping	
50 g (2 oz) butter	*12·5 g (½ oz) grated Parmesan cheese*
50 g (2 oz) finely grated Cheddar cheese	*1 level tbsp cornflour*

Heat the oven to 190° C (375° F), gas mark 5.

Put the lamb on a board and then cut the garlic into thin slivers and stick into the meat, rub over with butter. Place on a large piece of foil and pour over 150 ml (5 fl oz) cider. Lightly seal the foil and then place in a baking tin and roast in the oven for 30 minutes for each 450 g (1 lb). When half cooked, open the foil and baste frequently until the meat is tender. Remove from the oven and cool slightly, then put on a dish to carve and strain the juice from the foil, leave to cool and remove any excess fat.

Meanwhile prepare the stuffing. Finely chop the mushrooms; melt the butter in a pan, add the onion and fry for 3–4 minutes, add the mushrooms with the herbs and cook for 5 minutes, then stir in the breadcrumbs and seasoning and mix well. Leave to cool.

Carefully slice the lamb and insert a portion of stuffing between each slice, reshape and place back in the meat tin. Cream the butter and cheeses together and spread over the meat. Return to the oven for a further 25–30 minutes or until hot through.

To make a gravy, put a level tbsp cornflour in a small pan and stir in the cooled meat juices and the remaining cider; bring to boil, stirring until thickened. Cook for a minute and serve with the joint.

Steak au poivre   *Serves 4*

This classic way of serving steak is always prepared with whole black peppercorns, which are crushed in a mortar with a pestle, or if you have not got one, use a rolling pin on a firm board.

4 portions rump steak	*2 tbsp brandy*
2 level tbsp whole black peppercorns	*150 ml (5 fl oz) double cream*
50 g (2 oz) butter	*Salt*
1 tbsp oil	

Trim any excess fat or gristle from the steaks.

Crush the peppercorns coarsely in a mortar or with a rolling pin on a board, then with the fingers press the peppercorns into the steaks on both sides. Heat the butter and oil in a thick frying pan and cook the steaks on a high heat for 2 minutes just to seal the juices, turning once. Then lower the heat and cook the steaks for about 5 minutes for rare, 8 minutes for medium and 10–12 for well done. Lift out and place on a warm serving dish.

Add the brandy to the pan and, if liked, ignite when hot; as soon as the flames have gone, take the pan from the heat and stir in the cream, taste and season with salt if necessary and pour over the steaks. Serve at once.

A green salad or broccoli goes well with steak and as a change serve croquette potatoes.

Pepperpot beef   *Serves 8*

A perfect dish for informal entertaining; goes best with just a green salad of celery, avocado pear, chicory, raw green pepper and a little apple.

175 g (6 oz) dried red kidney beans	*3 good pinches ground ginger*
2 good pinches bicarbonate of soda	*1·1 kg (2½ lb) shin of beef cut into*
40 g (1½ oz) flour	*2·5 cm (1 in) cubes*
1½ tsp salt	*75 g (3 oz) dripping*
Pepper	

Sauce

A few drops of tabasco sauce	*3 tbsp cider vinegar*
397 g (14 oz) can peeled tomatoes	*2 cloves garlic, crushed*
300 ml (10 fl oz) stock	*1 bay leaf*
3 tbsp soft brown sugar	*1 red pepper*
225 g (8 oz) mushrooms, sliced	

Place the kidney beans in a basin with the bicarbonate of soda, cover with cold water and leave to stand overnight; drain.

Heat the oven to 160° C (325° F), gas mark 3.

Mix the flour, seasoning and ginger together and coat the meat thoroughly; melt the dripping in a frying pan and fry the meat quickly to brown, then lift out with a slotted spoon and place in a large casserole with the beans. Combine all the sauce ingredients, except the red pepper, in the pan and bring to the boil. Pour over the meat, cover the casserole and cook in the oven for 2½–3 hours.

Remove the seeds and white pith from the red pepper and cut into rings. Add to the casserole, return to the oven and cook for a further 30 minutes; taste and check seasoning and remove the bay leaf.

Shobdon beef   *Serves 6*

Although this is technically a casserole it is special enough to serve for a dinner party. It is important to note that all spoon measures for this are level. Add the cream and horseradish just before serving, otherwise it will separate, giving the sauce an unattractive appearance. I thoroughly recommend this dish as being untemperamental and really different.

900 g (2 lb) chuck steak	*2 tsp salt*
40 g (1½ oz) beef dripping	*Ground black pepper*
1 large onion, chopped	*1 tsp sugar*
1 tsp curry powder	*1 tbsp Worcestershire sauce*
1 tsp ground ginger	*150 ml (5 fl oz) soured cream*
50 g (2 oz) flour	*2 tbsp bottled horseradish cream*
450 ml (15 fl oz) water	*Fresh chopped parsley to garnish*

Heat the oven to 160° C (325° F), gas mark 3.

Cut the meat into 1·8 cm (¾ in) cubes. Melt the dripping in a large pan, add the meat and brown on all sides. Add onion and turn in the the the dripping, then add the spices and flour and mix well. Stir in the water and bring to the boil, season well and add the sugar and Worcestershire sauce. Transfer to a casserole, cover and cook in the oven from 2½–3 hours or until the beef is tender.

Just before serving mix the cream with the horseradish and stir into the casserole. Sprinkle with parsley and serve.

Turkey en croûte   *Serves 6–8*

A real party dish and so easy to carve. Buy a boneless turkey roast from a good supermarket – usually available at the end of the week.

1 boneless turkey roast weighing about 775 g (1¾ lb)

Stuffing

1 onion, chopped	*¼ level tsp dried thyme*
25 g (1 oz) butter	*227 g (8 oz) packet puff pastry, thawed*
100 g (4 oz) mushrooms, chopped	*1 beaten egg*
Salt and pepper	

Sauce

25 g (1 oz) butter	*300 ml (10 fl oz) stock*
100 g (4 oz) mushrooms, sliced	*4 tbsp sherry*
19·5 g (¾ oz) flour	

If liked remove some of the thin string from the turkey roast, leaving just sufficient to hold the meat firmly in a roll.

Cook the onion in a small pan with the butter for 5 minutes and then add the mushrooms, seasoning and thyme and cook gently for 3–4 minutes or until the mushrooms are just cooked. Leave to cool.

Roll out the pastry to a square four times wider than the roll and a little longer. Place the stuffing in the centre of the pastry and lay the roll on top. Brush the edges with beaten egg and then fold over neatly to cover the turkey and seal the ends, trimming off any spare pastry which can then be rolled out and used to make leaves to decorate the top.

Chill in the refrigerator and then bake at 200° C (400° F), gas mark 6 for about 1¼ hours, having glazed the pastry with beaten egg so that it will be golden brown and shiny.

Meanwhile make the sauce. Melt the butter in a small pan and add the mushrooms and cook for 5 minutes, stir in the flour and blend well and then add the stock and bring to the boil, stirring, and simmer until thickened. Add the sherry and any juices from the meat and season to taste. Serve in a sauce boat with the turkey. Remove any string as the meat is carved.

Pork à l'orange   *Serves 6*

Use pork slices for this recipe; most butchers will cut you slices of pork from the top of the leg or spare rib. These cuts are tender and less expensive than pork fillet.

6 pork slices
2 large carrots, cut in thin strips
2 oranges
3 tbsp oil
2 large onions, chopped

50 g (2 oz) flour
450 ml (15 fl oz) stock
Salt and pepper
5 tbsp sherry

Heat the oven to 180° C (350° F), gas mark 4.

Fry the pork slices in their own fat for 2–3 minutes on each side until brown and then lift out and lay in an ovenproof dish. Put the carrots on top.

Grate the rind and squeeze the juice from the oranges.

Heat the oil in the pan and fry the onion for about 5 minutes until soft but not brown. Stir in the flour and cook for a minute. Add the stock, orange juice and rind, seasoning and sherry and bring to the boil, stirring until thickened. Pour over the pork and cook in the oven for 1–1½ hours or until the meat is tender. Serve with broccoli and new potatoes.

Pork with mustard cream sauce   *Serves 6*

A very special dish, ideal for a dinner party. The mustard in the sauce gives the dish a very special flavour.

50 g (2 oz) butter
6 pork slices
1 onion, very finely chopped
40 g (1½ oz) flour
450 ml (15 fl oz) chicken stock
150 ml (5 fl oz) white wine

Salt
Freshly ground black pepper
225 g (8 oz) mushrooms, sliced
150 ml (5 fl oz) double cream
1–2 tbsp Meaux mustard

Melt the butter in a large pan and fry the pork and onion until lightly browned; lift out the pork and place on one side. Stir the flour into the butter in the pan and cook for a minute. Add the stock and white wine with seasoning and bring to the boil, stirring until thickened; return the pork slices to the pan, cover and simmer until tender for about 30–40 minutes. Then add the mushrooms and cook for a further 10 minutes.

Meanwhile put the cream and mustard into a small saucepan and bring to the boil, stirring, remove from the heat and stir into the pork mixture, serve at once.

MEALS IN UNDER AN HOUR

The keenest and most dedicated cook does not always have hours to spend in the kitchen. Working wives have to come home in the evening and produce a meal quickly – and look as though they were enjoying it. Guests turn up unexpectedly. Mothers have hungry children back from school and demanding to be fed at once because they have to be at the youth club meeting in half an hour, or at the drama club or the music society rehearsal, and hadn't they warned you?

So it's as well to have some quick ideas in mind. All these dishes here can be prepared and cooked ready to eat in less than one hour. Some appear to be elaborate and will add to your reputation as a hostess, others are plain and good and ought to satisfy the most demanding family.

The wise cook will have a stock of the basics – bacon, cheese, eggs – in addition to the leftovers in the fridge. Or she may well have stopped on the way home to stock up with liver, meat, kidneys and chicken joints as required. Rice or noodles are quick and easy to cook and go towards making a filling meal in the shortest possible time.

Devilled kidneys   *Serves 4*

Simple to make, this is good when served with buttered noodles and crisp bacon rashers and, if liked, a few whole grilled mushrooms.

12 lamb's kidneys
12·5 g (½ oz) seasoned flour
25 g (1 oz) butter
1 onion, chopped
150 ml (5 fl oz) red wine

1 rounded tsp tomato purée
1 rounded tsp made mustard
2 tsp Worcestershire sauce
¼ tsp cayenne pepper
Salt

Cut the kidneys in half and remove the thin membrane and cores and then coat in the flour.

Melt the butter in a frying pan, add the onion and fry gently for 5 minutes. Add the kidneys and fry gently for 3 minutes, turning. Then blend in the remaining ingredients and bring to the boil. Reduce the heat and simmer gently for 10 minutes.

Taste and check seasoning and serve.

Scottish collops   *Serves 4*

Cold lamb is not very exciting, so this recipe makes the most of the leftover pieces from a large joint.

350 g (12 oz) cooked lamb
1 onion
25 g (1 oz) butter
25 g (1 oz) flour
150 ml (5 fl oz) stock

Salt and pepper
1 egg, beaten
Brown breadcrumbs
Shallow fat or oil for frying

Remove any fat or very hard pieces from the lamb and then mince and put on one side. Then mince the onion.

Melt the butter in a saucepan and add the onion, cover and cook gently for about 5–8 minutes or until the onion is soft but not brown. Stir in the flour and cook for a minute. Stir in the stock and bring to the boil, stirring until thickened, then season very well and add the minced lamb, mix thoroughly and leave on one side until cold.

Divide the mixture into 8 and with wetted hands shape into cakes. Then dip in the beaten egg and browned breadcrumbs and pat well to coat thoroughly. Put on a plate and leave in a cool place until required or until quite firm before frying.

Shallow fry in fat or oil for about 3–4 minutes on each side over a moderate heat turning once and then lift out and drain on kitchen paper.

Serve with jacket potatoes and leeks.

Beefburgers with Italian sauce   *Serves 4*

The sauce makes a delicious accompaniment to the beefburgers; serve with creamy mashed potato and a green vegetable or salad.

Sauce
1 tbsp oil
2 onions, chopped
1 clove garlic, crushed
1 green pepper, cut in strips

397 g (14 oz) can peeled tomatoes
1 level tsp dried oregano
Salt and pepper

Beefburgers
350 g (12 oz) good quality minced beef
100 gm (4 oz) beef sausagemeat
1 onion, grated

1 level tsp salt
Ground black pepper

First prepare the sauce. Heat the oil in a small pan and add the onions and garlic and fry for 5 minutes. Add the remaining ingredients and simmer gently for a further 15–20 minutes whilst making the beefburgers.

Place the beef, sausagemeat, onion and seasoning in a bowl and blend well together. With lightly floured hands shape the mixture into 8 balls and then flatten each out to a 7·5 cm (3 in) beefburger. Grill or fry in a very little dripping for about 2½–3 minutes on each side. Lift out and drain well and then place on a serving dish and serve the sauce spooned on top.

Clare's liver   *Serves 4*

You may well laugh at the name, but this is one of Clare's special recipes!

450 g (1 lb) lamb's liver
225 g (8 oz) onions

50 g (2 oz) dripping
50 g (2 oz) flour

Navarin of lamb (page 56)

600 ml (1 pt) beef stock
3 tbsp tomato ketchup
A good pinch dried marjoram

A few drops of Worcestershire sauce
Salt and pepper

Cut the liver into long, thin strips. Peel and very finely slice the onions. Melt the dripping in a pan, add the onions and fry for 5–10 minutes until the onions are golden brown. Stir in the flour and cook for 2 minutes, add the stock and bring to the boil, stirring until thickened. Add the ketchup, marjoram, Worcestershire sauce and seasoning, stir well, cover the pan and simmer the sauce for 20 minutes.

Add the liver to the sauce, stir lightly and then simmer for about 10 minutes or until just tender – do not overcook.

Serve with creamed potatoes, and sprouts or cabbage.

Kidneys hongroise   *Serves 4*

A rich way of serving kidneys, served ideally with noodles to sop up the sauce, or maybe rice.

8–10 lamb's kidneys
2 tbsp oil
25 g (1 oz) butter
1 onion, chopped
1 tbsp paprika pepper
25 g (1 oz) flour

300 ml (10 fl oz) stock
5 tbsp sherry
1 tsp tomato purée
Salt and pepper
100 g (4 oz) small button mushrooms
4 tbsp soured cream

Cut the kidneys in half and remove the thin membrane and cores and then cut each kidney half in 2 or 3 slices.

Heat the oil and butter in a frying pan and fry the onion and kidneys for 2–3 minutes, sprinkle in the paprika pepper and flour and cook for a further minute. Blend in the stock, sherry, tomato purée and season well and then bring to the boil, stirring until thickened. Add the mushroom and simmer very gently for about 5 minutes or until the kidneys are just tender.

Taste and check seasoning, stir in the cream and serve with noodles.

Kidneys Jerez   *Serves 4*

Take care not to overcook the kidneys otherwise they will go hard. Serve with freshly boiled white rice.

12 lamb's kidneys
2 tbsp oil
2 shallots, chopped
1 small clove garlic, crushed
1 level tbsp flour

150 ml (5 fl oz) stock
Salt and pepper
25 g (1 oz) butter
5 tbsp sherry

Braised beef in red wine (page 60)

Cut the kidneys in half and remove the thin membrane and cores, then cut each half into 3 slices.

Heat the oil in a small pan and add the shallots and garlic and fry for about 5 minutes until the shallots are soft. Stir in the flour and cook for a further minute, then gradually blend in the stock, stirring and cook until the sauce thickens and comes to the boil, then simmer for 3 minutes.

Heat the butter in a frying pan, season the kidneys and add to the pan and fry for about 5 minutes, turning to brown on all sides. Lift out the kidneys with a slotted spoon and add the sherry and shallot sauce to the juices in the pan, blend well and bring to the boil, stirring, Return the kidneys to the pan and heat through gently; taste and check seasoning and serve with rice.

Liver stroganoff   *Serves 4*

Good quality liver is essential for this recipe, as the cooking time is very short.

450 g (1 lb) calf's or lamb's liver
25 g (1 oz) flour
75 g (3 oz) butter
2 onions, chopped
175 g (6 oz) button mushrooms,
 sliced

4 tomatoes, skinned, seeded and
 chopped
Salt
Freshly ground black pepper
150 ml (5 fl oz) carton soured cream
Chopped parsley to garnish

Cut the liver in thin strips of 5 × 1·25 cm (2 × ½ in) and lightly coat in flour.

Melt half the butter in a frying pan and add the onion and fry for about 5 minutes or until soft. Add the mushrooms and tomatoes and fry for a further 2–3 minutes to cook. Lift out with a slotted spoon and keep warm on one side.

Add the remaining butter to the pan and fry the liver quickly for 3–4 minutes, stirring all the time, until just cooked. Return the vegetables to the pan and season thoroughly. Lower the heat, stir in the soured cream and reheat but do not boil. Turn into a warm serving dish, sprinkle with parsley and serve at once with plain boiled rice and a vegetable dish such as ratatouille or a green salad.

Dijon pork chops   *Serves 4*

This recipe is easily adapted to serve any number of people and is an unusual way of serving pork chops.

4 lean pork chops
Dijon mustard

About 100 g (4 oz) soft brown sugar
2 small oranges

Heat the oven to 190° C (375° F), gas mark 5.

Trim any excess fat from the chops and spread each with mustard on both sides and then roll in the sugar until thoroughly coated, all over. Lay in a shallow ovenproof dish in a single layer.

Thinly slice the oranges and arrange them over the top of the chops. If the chops are very large it is a good idea to add a little extra orange juice. Bake uncovered in the oven for 30–40 minutes, basting occasionally until golden brown and syrupy.

Serve with broccoli and sauté potatoes.

Normandy pork   *Serves 4*

Apples, pork and cider blend naturally together. If you have some Calvados – apple brandy – add a couple of spoonfuls before serving.

4 spare rib pork chops	*Ground black pepper*
1 tbsp oil	*Salt*
2 medium onions, chopped	*2 cooking apples, peeled, cored and*
40 g (1½ oz) flour	*sliced*
450 ml (15 fl oz) dry cider	*3–4 tbsp single cream*

Trim the rind from the chops.

Heat the oil in a frying pan and fry the chops until brown on both sides, lift out and keep on one side. Add the onion to the pan and fry for about 3 minutes, stirring occasionally. Blend in the flour and cook for a minute, then stir in the cider and bring to the boil, stirring until thickened; season well.

Return the chops to the pan with the apples, cover the pan and simmer for 45 minutes or until the chops are tender. Lift out the chops and arrange on a serving dish, taste sauce and check seasoning and then stir in the cream and spoon over the chops.

Piquant chump chops   *Serves 4*

Choose large lamb chump chops or, if not available, use a couple of small loin chops.

4 lamb chump chops	*½ tsp ground ginger*
½ tsp each salt and pepper	*25 g (1 oz) butter*
½ tsp caster sugar	

Piquant sauce

1–2 tsp chilli sauce	*2 tbsp tomato ketchup*
1 tbsp mushroom ketchup	*1 tsp soy sauce*
1 tbsp Worcestershire sauce	*2 cloves garlic, crushed*
2 tsp sugar	*2 bay leaves*
2 tbsp vinegar	*4 sprigs of parsley to garnish*

Heat the oven to 190° C (375° F), gas mark 5.

Trim the chops carefully. Mix together the salt, pepper, sugar and ginger and rub over the chops. Lay in a baking tin and put in the oven until brown on both sides.

Meanwhile mix together all the ingredient for the sauce. When the chops are brown, pour off all the fat from the baking tin, pour over the sauce and cover the tin with a lid of foil. Bake in the oven for 20–30 minutes, basting occasionally, until tender.

Arrange the chops on a serving dish and spoon over the sauce, removing the bay leaves. Garnish with sprigs of parsley on each chop.

Lamb chops ratatouille   *Serves 4*

Make this in the summer when tomatoes and courgettes are at their best.

1 small aubergine	*1 red pepper*
4 courgettes	*1 clove garlic, crushed*
Salt	*350 g (12 oz) tomatoes*
50 g (2 oz) butter	*Ground black pepper*
2 onions, sliced	*4 lamb chops*
1 green pepper	

Cut the aubergine and courgettes into 1·25 cm ($\frac{1}{2}$ in) slices, put on kitchen paper, sprinkle with salt and leave to stand for 30 minutes. Meanwhile heat the butter in a pan, add the onions and cook very slowly until they are soft but not coloured. Remove the seeds from the peppers and cut into thin strips.

Dry the aubergines and courgettes carefully with more kitchen paper and add to the pan with the peppers and garlic, cover and cook gently for 30 minutes, stirring occasionally.

Heat a moderate grill, place lamb chops on a grill rack and dot with a little butter and then grill for about 15 minutes, turning once.

Put the tomatoes in a bowl, cover with boiling water and leave to stand for 10 seconds. Drain and then peel, quarter and remove the seeds. Stir into the pan and cook gently for about 5 minutes, taste and season well.

Put the ratatouille on a serving dish and arrange the chops on top.

Gammon with pineapple and mustard   *Serves 4*

Use thick gammon rashers for this recipe and trim off the rind.

4 thick gammon rashers	*3 level tbsp demerara sugar*
1 level tbsp dry mustard	*227 g (8 oz) can pineapple rings*

Trim the rind and any excess fat from the rashers and snip the edges to stop them curling up.

Blend the mustard and sugar together in a bowl and add sufficient pineapple juice to make a thin glaze.

Heat the grill to moderate, lay the gammon rashers in the pan and pour over the glaze; grill for about 5 minutes on each side, turning once. Place a pineapple ring on each gammon rasher and heat for a minute. Then place on a warm serving dish and pour over the juices from the pan.

Lamb foil parcels   *Serves 4*

Serve with rice or mashed potatoes, best made when tomatoes are cheap and in season, but if very expensive use canned tomatoes with their juice.

4 chump chops	*350 g (12 oz) tomatoes, skinned and*
25 g (1 oz) flour	*quartered*
12·5 g (½ oz) dripping	*¼ level tsp mixed herbs*
1 large onion, chopped	*Salt and pepper*
1 clove garlic, crushed	

Heat the oven to 190° C (375° F), gas mark 5.

Coat the chops in flour, having trimmed off any excess fat. Heat the dripping in a frying pan and fry the chops quickly until golden brown on both sides. Lift out and place on a 25 cm (10 in) square of foil. Add the onion and garlic to the dripping in the pan and cook until soft – about 5 minutes – then blend in the onion, garlic, tomatoes and herbs and season well, cook for 2 minutes and then divide the mixture between the four chops.

Fold over the foil and seal firmly and place on a baking tray and bake in the oven for 30–45 minutes depending on how thick the chops are; serve straight from the foil packet.

Hungarian mince   *Serves 4*

A very tasty way of serving pie veal – the noodles have a lovely flavour and appearance.

Sauce

25 g (1 oz) butter	*1 level tbsp paprika pepper*
2 onions, finely chopped	*25 g (1 oz) flour*
450 g (1 lb) pie veal, minced	*1 level tbsp tomato purée*
Salt and pepper	*300 ml (10 fl oz) dry cider or stock*

Noodles

225 g (8 oz) egg noodles	*1 green pepper, blanched and cut in*
50 g (2 oz) butter	*thin strips*

2–3 tbsp soured cream

Melt the butter in a saucepan, add the onions and fry gently until a pale golden brown. Add the veal and fry, stirring for a few minutes, then stir in the salt and pepper, paprika and flour and cook for a minute. Add tomato purée and cider and bring to the boil, stirring. Cover the pan and simmer for 30–45 minutes or until veal is tender.

Meanwhile cook the noodles as directed on the packet in plenty of boiling salted water; drain thoroughly. Rinse out the pan and add the butter and green pepper and heat thoroughly, then stir in the noodles until lightly coated with melted butter, taste and check seasoning and add plenty of freshly ground black pepper. Spoon the noodles in a border around the edge of a warm serving dish.

Stir the soured cream into the veal, taste and check seasoning, and spoon into the centre of the noodles.

Beef curry   *Serves 4*

This is an ideal way of using up the last of the Sunday joint. If you don't have beef use lamb or pork.

25 g (1 oz) dripping	*1 rounded tbsp mango chutney*
1 large onion	*350 g (12 oz) leftover cooked beef*
2 sticks celery	*Salt*
1 level tbsp curry powder	
25 g (1 oz) flour	
450 ml (15 fl oz) beef stock or gravy from the joint	
1 level tbsp tomato purée	

Melt the dripping in a pan, peel and chop the onion and slice the celery, add to the dripping in the pan and cook gently for 10 minutes or until the onion is soft. Stir in the curry powder and cook for 2–3 minutes, add the flour and mix well.

Stir in the stock or gravy and bring to the boil, stirring; add the tomato purée and chutney, cover and simmer for about 30 minutes.

Add the meat cut in neat pieces, add salt to taste and simmer for a further 10 minutes. Serve with plain boiled rice and if liked side dishes of chutney, poppadums, bananas, peanuts and sliced tomatoes and onions.

Lemon baked chicken   *Serves 4*

This is a simple way of cooking chicken that gives it a lovely flavour. The recipe is easily adapted for any number of portions.

4 chicken joints	*Salt and freshly ground black pepper*
2 tbsp oil	*Juice of 1 small lemon*
4 tomatoes, peeled and thickly sliced	*4 rashers lean streaky bacon*

Heat the oven to 180° C (350° F), gas mark 4.

Remove the skin from the chicken joints. Heat the oil in a frying pan and fry the joints until lightly brown. Lay the tomatoes in a single layer in the base of a shallow ovenproof dish and then put the chicken on top in a single layer; season well.

Pour the lemon juice over, remove the rind and any small pieces of bone from the bacon and arrange a rasher on top of each joint.

Cover the dish and bake in the oven for about 40 minutes or until the chicken is tender. Serve with new potatoes and a green salad or vegetable – such as broccoli.

Meat balls in sweet and sour sauce   *Serves 4*

A very tasty way to serve mince, a great favourite in our house.

450 g (1 lb) raw minced beef
75 g (3 oz) fresh white breadcrumbs
1 egg
Salt and pepper
2 tbsp oil
1 onion, chopped
2 carrots, cut in thin strips
1 leek, finely sliced

50 g (2 oz) mushrooms, sliced
1 level tbsp cornflour
2 tsp brown sugar
300 ml (10 fl oz) water
2 tbsp tomato ketchup
1 tbsp vinegar
1 tbsp soy sauce
Salt and pepper

Put the beef, breadcrumbs, egg and seasoning in a bowl and mix well. Turn onto a floured surface and shape into 20 meat balls.

Heat the oil in a pan and fry the meat balls until brown all over, lift out with a slotted spoon and put on one side. Add the vegetables to the pan and fry slowly for 3–4 minutes.

Place all the remaining ingredients in a bowl and blend well. Add to the pan and bring to the boil, stirring until thickened. Return the meat balls to the pan, cover and simmer for about 40 minutes or until tender.

Taste and check seasoning and serve with noodles.

Sausages boulangère   *Serves 4*

Try serving sausages this way next time they are on the menu. Once prepared it is only necessary to cook a vegetable to make this a complete meal.

A very little oil
450 g (1 lb) pork sausages
675 g (1½ lb) potatoes, peeled and thinly
 sliced
1 large onion, chopped

Salt and pepper
1 tbsp fresh chopped herbs
300 ml (10 fl oz) milk
1 chicken stock cube

Heat the oven to 180° C (350° F), gas mark 4 and butter a shallow ovenproof dish.

Heat the oil in a frying pan and fry the sausages until brown all over; this will take about 5 minutes.

Mix potatoes with the onion and put in the dish, seasoning well; sprinkle with herbs. Lay the sausages on top.

Rinse out the frying pan, add the milk and stock cube and bring to the boil, stirring until the cube has dissolved; pour over the potatoes. Cover the dish with foil and cook in the oven for 30 minutes, then remove the foil and cook for a further 20 minutes or until the potatoes are soft.

Crunchy cabbage with pork ring   *Serves 4*

Smoked pork ring is mildly smoky and special. I like to add thick slices to a tasty vegetable soup to make it a main meal.

50 g (2 oz) butter
2 large onions, sliced
1 clove garlic, crushed
225 g (8 oz) carrots, thinly sliced
2 levels tsp curry powder
1 tbsp soy sauce
¾ level tsp salt

Freshly ground black pepper
350 g (12 oz) white cabbage, finely shredded
225 g (8 oz) peas
240 g (8½ oz) smoked pork sausage, thickly sliced

Heat the butter in a large frying pan and add the onions, garlic and carrots and cook gently for 8 minutes, stirring. Then add the curry powder, soy sauce, salt and pepper; stir in the cabbage and mix thoroughly, cover the pan and cook over a low heat for about 12 minutes or until the carrots and cabbage are tender.

Meanwhile cook the peas in boiling salted water and then drain and stir into the cabbage mixture with the smoked pork sausage; heat through and then taste and check seasoning. Serve at once.

Bacon, kidney and sausage kebabs   *Makes 4 kebabs*

These are simple kebabs that the children can make themselves.

6 rashers streaky bacon   *4 chipolata sausages*   *4 lamb's kidneys*

Baste
1 tsp tomato ketchup   *1 tsp Worcestershire sauce*   *1 tbsp oil*

Preheat the grill or, in summer, a barbecue.

Remove the rind from the bacon and stretch the bacon flat with the back of a knife. Cut each rasher in half and roll up. Twist each sausage in two and separate. Skin the kidneys, cut in half and remove the cores.

Oil 4 skewers and on each put 3 bacon rolls, 2 pieces of kidney and 2 small sausages.

Mix all the baste ingredients together and brush over the kebabs and grill for about 10–12 minutes on a medium grill; brush with more baste and turn during cooking.

Serve with long rolls, savoury rice or mixed salads.

Chinese pork kebabs   *Makes 4 kebabs*

A slightly more sophisticated kebab, that adults will enjoy.

2 tbsp soy sauce	*3 tbsp water*
1 tsp sugar	*450 g (1 lb) pork fillet*
2 tbsp sherry	*4 small onions, quartered*

Blend the soy sauce, sugar, sherry and water together. Cut the pork fillet into 2·5 cm (1 in) cubes and put in a dish with the sauce mixture, cover and leave in a cool place for several hours.

Preheat the grill or barbecue.

Thread the meat, alternating with quarters of onions on 4 well oiled skewers. Grill for about 15 minutes, turning and basting during cooking. Serve with a savoury rice.

Lamb kebabs   *Makes 4 kebabs (See colour plate facing page 48)*

Serve these kebabs with a crisp green salad and plain boiled rice for an easy meal.

450 g (1 lb) lamb from leg or shoulder

Marinade

2 tbsp oil	*1 onion, roughly chopped*
1 tbsp vinegar	*Salt and pepper*
1 clove garlic, crushed	

4 tomatoes, halved	*2 small onions, sliced*
8 button mushrooms	*1 green pepper, cut in 8 and de-seeded*
4 lambs' kidneys, halved	*Chopped parsley to garnish*

Cut the lamb into 2·5 cm (1 in) cubes and put in a bowl. Blend the marinade ingredients together and pour over the lamb, cover and leave in a cool place to marinade, preferably overnight.

Heat the grill to moderate.

Thread the pieces of lamb on 4 lightly oiled long skewers with the halved tomatoes, mushrooms, kidneys, onions and pieces of green pepper. Brush with a little marinade and then grill for about 10–12 minutes, turning until the meat is tender. Sprinkle with chopped parsley.

HOME-MADE PATES

For a sophisticated summer lunch party you could serve a subtly flavoured pâté with thin slices of brown bread and butter and a variety of salads; for a family picnic, hearty slices of home-made pâté with wholemeal bread and butter; and a selection of different pâtés with a variety of breads and biscuits could be the basis of a buffet supper.

Made in an electric blender pâté is quick and easy to prepare. Make fish pâtés a quantity at a time and store what you do not use at once – it freezes well. Meat pâtés I find really are best stored in the freezer for up to 3 weeks only. Smoked fish such as kippers, bloaters or mackerel need only a squeeze of lemon juice for added flavour. Cream and brandy go into an extravagant pâté, garlic into a strongly flavoured one.

Presentation is important; it is worth paying attention to appearance. An attractive pot or terrine and a colourful garnish of parsley, watercress, tomato or lemon slices; add hot toast in a napkin, crisp rolls, wholemeal bread and unsalted butter, a bottle of wine . . . there's a meal fit for a discerning gourmet.

Buckling pâté   *Serves 6*

Smoked trout can be used for this recipe as well. Smoked buckling are herrings smoked for a long time at a moderately high temperature. The smoking process is very similar to the one used for smoking trout, so buckling doesn't need cooking. Serve as you would smoked trout, with horseradish cream or made into this creamy piquant pâté. Make in an electric blender if you prefer (it will mix smoother if the butter is melted first), then chill till set before serving. It is quite a good idea to buy more buckling than you need for one occasion, as not all fish shops sell it; it freezes very well.

2 large buckling
100 gm (4 oz) softened butter
2 crushed cloves garlic (optional)

2 tbsp lemon juice
Freshly ground pepper

Drop the buckling into boiling water for a minute, then skin and bone. Pound the flesh with a wooden spoon and blend together with the butter, add the garlic, lemon juice and pepper and mix well.

Turn into a dish, smooth the top and serve with hot toast.

Good kipper pâté   *Serves 6*

Inexpensive to make and full of flavour.

170 g (6 oz) packet frozen buttered
  kipper fillets
2 tsp lemon juice

150 ml (5 fl oz) whipping cream,
  whipped
Salt and pepper

Cook the kipper fillets in the bag according to the directions on the packet. Open the bag, reserve the juices and peel off the kipper skins. Purée the kippers in a blender with the juices, or mash with a fork until smooth.

When the paste is cold, stir in the lemon juice and mix well and then stir in the cream, taste and check seasoning. Turn into a dish and smooth the top and chill in the refrigerator. Remove 1 hour before required.

Bloater pâté   *Serves 6*

Bloaters have very much gone out of fashion, but they are full of flavour and available from good fishmongers. Add lots of lemon and ground black pepper. Serve with hot brown rolls and celery for an informal lunch.

2 bloaters, cleaned   *Juice of half a lemon*
275 g (10 oz) butter, melted but not hot   *Freshly ground black pepper*
100 g (4 oz) cream cheese   *Parsley or watercress to garnish*

Put the bloaters under a hot grill and brush with a little of the butter and cook for about 3 minutes on each side. Remove from the pan and lift off the skin and remove any bones, then put in a bowl with 225 g (8 oz) of the butter, the cream cheese, lemon juice and pepper. Divide the mixture in half and put in the blender in 2 batches and blend until smooth. Put in a small tureen or dish about 600 ml (1 pt) size.

Pour over the remaining butter and leave in a cool place until set. Serve garnished with small sprigs of parsley or watercress.

Pâté loaf   *Serves 6*

This is really a cross between the pâté and a meat loaf. Serve cut in slices with a green salad. Make the bread from the inside of the loaf into breadcrumbs and use for stuffing.

1 small brown loaf   *½ tsp mixed dried herbs*
1 small onion, quartered   *½ tsp salt*
100 g (4 oz) pig's liver   *Freshly ground black pepper*
225 g (8 oz) pork sausagemeat   *3 tbsp sherry*
225 g (8 oz) minced beef

Heat the oven to 180° C (350° F), gas mark 4.

Cut a slice from the end of the loaf and scoop out the bread in the centre to leave about 1·25 cm (½ in) all round the edge.

Mince the onion and the liver and put in a bowl with all the remaining ingredients and mix thoroughly. Pack tightly into the loaf taking care not to break the bread case; replace the end slice. Lightly wrap the loaf in foil and bake in the centre of the oven for 1¼ hours and then open the foil and continue cooking for a further 30 minutes or until the meat is cooked.

Remove from the oven and leave to become quite cold and then serve sliced with a variety of salads.

Smooth pâté with brandy   *Serves 6–8*

Fine brandied liver pâté. Serve for a light smart lunch with brown bread rolls and unsalted butter.

450 g (1 lb) chicken livers	*3 tbsp brandy*	*Ground black pepper*
225 g (8 oz) butter	*Salt*	*A sprig of parsley to garnish*

Trim the livers if necessary. Melt half the butter in a frying pan, add the livers and fry gently for about 5 minutes. Remove from the pan and purée in a blender with the brandy until smooth.

Cream the remaining butter in a basin and add the liver mixture, beat thoroughly and season with salt and plenty of ground black pepper.

Turn into a dish and smooth the top and chill until firm.

Garnish the top with a sprig of parsley.

Brawn   *Serves 4*

If you buy a pig for the freezer it sometimes comes with the head and trotters and this is an excellent way of using them.

½ a pig's head cut into 2 or 3 pieces	*2 bay leaves*
2 pig's trotters	*6 peppercorns*
Salt and pepper	*6 cloves*
2 onions, quartered	*3 parsley sprigs*
1 large carrot, scraped and sliced	*Sliced tomatoes and watercress to garnish*

Put the head and trotters in a large bowl with a handful of salt. Cover with cold water and leave to soak for eight hours or overnight. Drain and place in a large saucepan. Cover with fresh cold water and bring to the boil, removing the scum. When the liquid is free of scum, add the onions, carrot, bay leaves, peppercorns and cloves. Cover and simmer for 2½ hours or until tender.

Remove the head and trotters from the pan and separate the meat from the skin and bones. Cut the meat into neat pieces and set aside. Discard the skin. Return the bones to the pan with 1 tsp of salt and boil rapidly until the cooking liquid has reduced to about 600 ml (1 pt), strain and set aside to become quite cold.

Chop the parsley and mix with the meat. Check the seasoning and turn into a pudding basin. Remove the fat from the cooled cooking liquor and blend with the meat; leave to set in the refrigerator.

To serve, turn out onto a serving dish and garnish with tomato slices and small sprigs of watercress.

PASTA, RICE AND PIZZAS

There is more to pasta than the good old standby spaghetti bolognese – and that takes a lot of beating. So does macaroni cheese. Pasta in all its forms, spaghetti, macaroni, vermicelli, lasagne, canneloni, noodles and so on, is the basis of an enormous number of dishes.

It is easy to cook, economical, filling. It makes a little meat go a long way; all that most pasta dishes need is a well-flavoured sauce and plenty of grated cheese. With a green salad and a glass of wine it can be a meal to be remembered. Pasta dishes are easy to serve and they freeze well if you are cooking ahead.

Pasta shells or noodles can take the place of potatoes. So can rice, which goes particularly well with chicken or fish. Rice, in the form of risotto or the classic Spanish paella can be a noble dish in its own right.

The Italians gave us pasta and they also gave us pizza with all its variations, colourful and rich with the flavours of tomato, cheese and herbs, a splendid food for parties.

Crisp supper dish   *Serves 4*

A great favourite in our household, all from ingredients in the store cupboard. A saver on the day when there has been no time to shop for family supper and the fridge is bare.

175 g (6 oz) pasta shells	*200 g (7 oz) can tuna fish*
Salt	*75 g (3 oz) Cheddar cheese, grated*
25 g (1 oz) margarine	*1 rounded tbsp chopped parsley*
25 g (1 oz) flour	*Pepper*
450 ml (15 fl oz) milk	*2 heaped tbsp fresh white breadcrumbs*

Heat the oven to 190° C (375° F), gas mark 5.

Cook the pasta shells in plenty of boiling salted water until tender. Drain and rinse well in warm water and then put on kitchen paper so that the pieces do not stick together.

Melt the margarine in a pan, add the flour and cook for 2 minutes, stir in the milk and bring to the boil; cook for 2 minutes.

Drain the liquor from the tuna and add to the sauce, then flake and stir into the sauce with 50 g (2 oz) of the cheese, parsley and seasoning to taste.

Layer the pasta shells and sauce in a generous 1 l (2 pt) shallow ovenproof dish starting with a layer of pasta and finishing with a layer of sauce. Sprinkle the top with the remaining cheese and breadcrumbs and bake in the oven for about 40 minutes until golden brown.

Serve with a green salad.

Italian meat balls   *Serves 4 (See cover photograph)*

A colourful dish that may be prepared in advance, and reheated when required in a moderate oven for about 45 minutes. It only needs a green vegetable to make the meal complete.

225 g (8 oz) good quality minced beef
225 g (8 oz) pork sausagemeat
½ tsp salt
Freshly ground black pepper
A little flour
2 tsbp oil
1 large onion, sliced
1 clove garlic, crushed
1 green pepper, de-seeded and sliced

3 tbsp tomato purée
150 ml (5 fl oz) cider
150 ml (5 fl oz) stock
100 g (4 oz) button mushrooms, sliced
A little sugar
Salt and freshly ground black pepper
225 g (8 oz) noodles
100 g (4 oz) Cheddar cheese, grated

Put the minced beef in a bowl with the sausagemeat, salt and pepper and blend together. Lightly flour your hands and divide the mixture into 24 pieces and roll into small balls on a lightly floured surface. Heat the oil in a large pan and add the meat balls, onion and garlic and fry quickly until golden brown. Add the green pepper, tomato purée, cider, stock and mushrooms and bring to the boil; add a little sugar and plenty of seasoning and then simmer for 20 minutes.

Meanwhile cook the noodles as directed on the packet and drain thoroughly. Stir in the sauce with the cheese until well mixed. Heat through gently and then taste and check seasoning. Serve with a green vegetable.

To freeze: cool, cover in a rigid container and label. To serve: leave to thaw at room temperature for about 8 hours, then turn into a casserole and heat in a moderate oven 180° C (350° F), gas mark 4 for about 1¼ hours, stirring occasionally.

Lasagne   *Serves 6*

No need to cook the pasta first in this lasagne, just layer it up with the two sauces which are made on the thin side and the pasta will cook, taking moisture from the two sauces.

Meat sauce
450 g (1 lb) minced beef
25 g (1 oz) streaky bacon, de-rinded
 and chopped
225 g (8 oz) onions, chopped
4 sticks celery, chopped
12·5 g (½ oz) flour
300 ml (10 fl oz) stock

90 g (3½ oz) can tomato purée
2 cloves garlic, crushed
2 tsp redcurrant jelly
½ tsp salt
Pepper
¼ tsp dried thyme

White sauce
40 g (1½ oz) butter
40 g (1½ oz) flour
¼ tsp nutmeg

Salt and pepper
600 ml (1 pt) milk
½ tsp made mustard

100 g (4 oz) Cheddar cheese, grated
100 g (4 oz) Emmenthal, grated

150 g (5 oz) uncooked lasagne
12·5 g (½ oz) Parmesan, grated

For the meat sauce: place the minced beef in the pan with the bacon and fry until browned and all the fat has run out. Add the onions and celery and cook for 5 minutes, stir in the remaining ingredients, bring to the boil, cover and simmer for 1 hour.

Now make the white sauce: melt the butter in a large pan and stir in the flour, nutmeg, salt and pepper and cook gently for 2 minutes. Remove the pan from the heat and gradually add the milk, stirring to make a smooth mixture. Return the pan to the heat and bring to the boil, stirring until the sauce has thickened; add the mustard and check seasoning.
Combine the Cheddar and Emmenthal cheese.

In a shallow 2 l (3½ pt) casserole put a third of the meat sauce, the white sauce and a third of the cheese, followed by half of the uncooked lasagne (lay edge to edge, not overlapping); break the pieces to fit the dish.

Then start again with a third of the meat sauce, white sauce and cheese and last half of the lasagne. Repeat, finishing with a final layer of meat sauce, white sauce and cheese and the grated Parmesan. Leave to become quite cold, then cook when required at 180° C (350° F), gas mark 4 for 45–60 minutes or until hot through and the top is golden brown and bubbling. Serve at once; if necessary keep in a cool oven for up to 1 hour.

Serve with garlic bread and a green salad.

This may be frozen: make in a foil container and then cool, cover, label and freeze. To serve, thaw overnight in the refrigerator and then bake.

American rice with chicken   *Serves 4*

A spicy rice mixture; you could use parboiled long grain rice for this recipe.

3–4 tbsp oil
4 chicken joints
1 onion, chopped
2 sticks celery, chopped
1 green or red pepper, de-seeded and
  cut in strips
225 g (8 oz) long grain rice
750 ml (1¼ pt) water
227 g (8 oz) can peeled tomatoes

1 chicken stock cube
1 clove garlic, crushed
¾ tsp curry powder
¼ tsp mixed dried herbs
¼ tsp chilli powder
50 g (2 oz) mushrooms, sliced
100 g (4 oz) frozen peas
Salt and pepper

Heat two-thirds of the oil in a pan and fry the chicken quickly until golden brown on both sides, then reduce the heat, cover and continue to cook until the joints are tender – about 20 minutes. Lift out of the pan and leave to drain on kitchen paper.

Add the onion, celery and pepper to the pan and fry for a few minutes until soft. Add the rice and fry for a further few minutes. Add water, tomatoes, stock cube, garlic, curry powder, herbs and chilli powder, bring to the boil, stir lightly and then cover and simmer for about 25 minutes, or until all the liquid has been absorbed and the rice cooked.

Slice the mushrooms and fry in a small pan in the remaining oil for a few minutes and then stir into the rice mixture with the chicken and peas. Reheat, stirring frequently and season to taste. Serve piping hot.

Pizzas   *Serves 4 each*

Make two pizzas at a time, one to eat now and one to freeze for another meal.

Yeast mixture
225 ml (7½ fl oz) hand-hot water
½ tsp sugar
1½ level tsp dried yeast

350 g (12 oz) strong bread flour
1½ level tsp salt
A knob of lard

Tomato and anchovy topping
397 g (14 oz) can peeled tomatoes,
 drained and roughly chopped
¼ tsp oregano

Salt and freshly ground black pepper
75 g (3 oz) Emmenthal cheese, sliced
Anchovy fillets

Mushroom and bacon topping
25 g (1 oz) butter
4 rashers streaky bacon, chopped

50 g (2 oz) button mushrooms, sliced
50 g (2 oz) Cheddar cheese, grated

First prepare the bread: dissolve the sugar in the water, sprinkle on the yeast and leave for 10–15 minutes until frothy. Put the flour in a large bowl with the salt and rub in the lard, pour on the yeast liquid and mix well to a dough that will leave the sides of the bowl clean.

Turn onto a floured table and knead until smooth and no longer sticky – this will take about 10 minutes – or until the dough is smooth and feels firm and elastic. Shape into a large ball, place in a polythene bag greased with a little oil, and leave in a warm place to rise until doubled in bulk. Turn onto a floured table and knead back to the original bulk and divide the dough into 2 equal portions and roll out to 20 cm (8 in) circles on a baking tray or foil dish and brush each with a little oil.

To make the tomato and anchovy topping: mix the tomatoes with the oregano and seasoning, spread over one dough circle, cover with cheese slices and arrange the anchovies in a lattice on top.

To make the mushroom and bacon topping: melt the butter in a small pan, add the bacon and mushrooms and cook together for 5 minutes, drain and arrange on the other piece of dough, sprinkle with the grated cheese.

Leave the pizzas in a warm place for about 20 minutes or until the dough is slightly puffy.

Bake in a hot oven 220° C (425° F), gas mark 7 for 20–25 minutes until the cheese is golden brown and bubbling and the dough is well risen and crisp.

Serve warm.

To freeze: leave the pizzas to prove in a warm place for 20 minutes and then open freeze until firm, then wrap in a double thickness of foil, label and return to the freezer. To serve: unwrap, place on a lightly oiled baking tray and bake in the oven as above but for 25–30 minutes.

Paella   *Serves 8*

A good dish for a crowd. By no means a budget recipe. It will keep quite well covered with foil for up to an hour in a cool oven.

5 tbsp oil	2 level tsp salt
450 g (1 lb) raw chicken on the bone, in small pieces	Plenty of ground black pepper
	450 g (1 lb) long grain rice
225 g (8 oz) bacon pieces, chopped	100 g (4 oz) peeled prawns
1 large onion, chopped	100 g (4 oz) frozen peas
2 cloves garlic, crushed	12 whole prawns in shell
225 g (8 oz) tomatoes, skinned, quartered and de-seeded	225 g (8 oz) green pepper, de-seeded and sliced
Scant 1 l (1½ pt) chicken stock	12 stuffed green olives
Thimble of saffron powder or ½ level tsp turmeric	Wedges of lemon
	Cooked mussels, if liked

Heat the oil in a paella pan, add the chicken and fry over a medium heat for about 15 minutes, turning until brown on all sides. Add the bacon and onion and fry for a further 5 minutes.

Stir in the garlic, tomatoes, stock and saffron and bring to the boil, add the salt and pepper and stir in the rice, peeled prawns and peas. Arrange the whole prawns and green pepper slices on top. Cover with a piece of foil and put in the oven at 180° C (350° F), gas mark 4 for about 45 minutes or until the rice is tender and the stock absorbed. Taste and check seasoning and decorate with stuffed green olives, lemon wedges, and mussels if liked.

Spaghetti bolognese   *Serves 4–6*

A firm favourite with young and old alike.

2 tbsp salad oil
225 g (8 oz) onions, chopped
2 sticks celery, sliced
450 g (1 lb) minced beef
A good 25 g (1 oz) flour
62 g (2½ oz) can tomato purée
2 cloves garlic, crushed
150 ml (5 fl oz) beef stock

150 ml (5 fl oz) red wine
397 g (14 oz) can tomatoes
1 tbsp red wine
1 level tsp salt
Freshly ground black pepper
350 g (12 oz) spaghetti
Parmesan cheese

Heat the oil in a pan and fry the onions, celery and minced beef for 5 minutes. Stir in the flour and tomato purée and garlic and cook for a minute. Add the stock, wine, tomatoes and seasoning and bring to the boil, stirring until thickened. Reduce the heat, partially cover the saucepan and simmer gently for about 1 hour or until the beef is tender.

Meanwhile cook the spaghetti in a pan of fast-boiling salted water for as long as directed on the packet. When ready the spaghetti should be slightly firm to the bite but not hard in the centre. Strain through a colander, rinse out with warm water. Rinse the pan, add a little oil or a large knob of butter and return the pasta to the pan and toss gently.

Serve the spaghetti onto plates, ladle the sauce on top and hand the cheese out separately.

Pot luck risotto   *Serves 4*

Chicken livers are suggested in this recipe but maybe you have the last cuts from the chicken that could be used instead.

4 rashers bacon
75 g (3 oz) butter
1 onion, chopped
225 g (8 oz) long grain rice
600 ml (1 pt) stock

Salt and pepper
225 g (8 oz) chicken livers
A little seasoned flour
100 g (4 oz) small whole mushrooms

Cut the rind from the bacon and cut into small pieces. Melt 25 g (1 oz) butter in a saucepan and add the onion and bacon, cover the pan and cook gently for about 5 minutes until the onion is soft but not brown.

Stir in the rice and cook for a minute, add the stock and bring to the boil, stirring all the time, add plenty of seasoning and then cover the pan and simmer for about 25–30 minutes or until the rice is tender and all the stock absorbed.

Meanwhile trim the chicken livers and cut into slices and coat in a little seasoned flour. Heat the remaining butter in a frying pan and fry the chicken livers with the mushrooms for about 5 minutes or until tender, stirring occasionally. Lightly stir into the rice with a fork.

Serve piled on a warm dish with a bowl of grated cheese and a green salad.

Old-fashioned macaroni cheese with bacon   *Serves 4*

A family supper dish for when funds are low and the fridge is bare. If everyone is very hungry surround the dish with fried bread croutons.

75 g (3 oz) short-cut macaroni   *Salt and pepper*
25 g (1 oz) butter   *100 g (4 oz) grated cheese*
25 g (1 oz) flour   *6 rashers streaky bacon*
450 ml (15 fl oz) milk

Cook the macaroni in boiling salted water until just tender, according to the directions on the packet (about 10 minutes). Drain and put on one side.

Melt the butter in a saucepan and stir in the flour and cook for a minute. Blend in the milk and bring to the boil, stirring until the sauce has thickened. Remove from the heat and add 75 g (3 oz) of the cheese and season well. Stir in the macaroni.

Pour into a buttered ovenproof dish and sprinkle with the remaining cheese. De-rind the bacon and cut each rasher in half, form into rolls and put on a tray.

Bake in the oven at 220° C (425° F), gas mark 7 for about 15 minutes or until hot through and golden brown. Arrange the bacon rolls around the edge of the macaroni.

Italian chicken with noodle shells   *Serves 4*

Serve with a bright green vegetable such as French beans or broccoli – no need to serve potatoes.

4 chicken joints   *25 g (1 oz) flour*
25 g (1 oz) butter   *150 ml (5 fl oz) red wine*
100 g (4 oz) piece smoked streaky *150 ml (5 fl oz) chicken stock*
* bacon, diced*   *Salt and freshly ground black pepper*
1 onion, chopped   *100 g (4 oz) noodle shells*
1 clove garlic, crushed

Heat the oven to 160° C (325° F), gas mark 3.

Remove the skin from the chicken. Melt the butter in a pan and fry the chicken until brown, lift out and place in a casserole.

Add the bacon to the fat remaining in pan with the onion and garlic and fry until it is brown and the onion is soft. Stir in the flour and cook for 2 minutes. Add the wine, stock and seasoning and bring to the boil, pour over the chicken joints and then cover with a tight fitting lid and cook in the oven for 45 minutes.

Meanwhile cook the noodle shells as directed on the packet until they are *al dente* (just cooked with a slight bite in the centre), drain and rinse well and then stir into the casserole. Return to the oven and cook for a further 10–15 minutes or until the chicken is tender and the shells are hot through.

Canneloni   *Serves 4*

Canneloni makes a very good supper or lunch dish when filled with a savoury meat sauce like this, serve with a dressed green salad; no potatoes or bread are necessary.

Filling
225 g (8 oz) minced beef   *1 level tbsp flour*
1 large onion, chopped   *150 ml (5 fl oz) beef stock*
1 clove garlic, crushed   *Salt and pepper*
2 tsp tomato purée   *8 sticks no-cook canneloni*

Cheese sauce
25 g (1 oz) butter   *1 level tsp made English mustard*
25 g (1 oz) flour   *Salt and pepper*
450 ml (15 fl oz) milk   *75 g (3 oz) Cheddar cheese*

Put the beef, onion and garlic in a small saucepan and fry gently for about 5 minutes or until the fat runs out. Stir in the tomato purée and flour and cook for a minute, blend in the stock and seasoning and then bring to the boil, stirring. Reduce the heat and simmer, partially covered, for about 30 minutes or until beef is tender. Remove from heat, taste and check seasoning and then leave to cool. When cold fill into the raw canneloni.

Now make the sauce; melt the butter in a pan and stir in the flour and cook for a minute, add the milk and bring to the boil, stirring until thickened, add the mustard and seasoning and simmer for 2 minutes. Stir in 50 g (2 oz) of the cheese.

Place a thin layer of sauce in the bottom of a shallow ovenproof dish and lay the canneloni on top in a single layer and then spoon over the remaining sauce and sprinkle with the last of the cheese.

Bake in the oven for 35–40 minutes at 190° C (375° F), gas mark 5 or until golden brown and bubbling and the canneloni is tender.

Savoury brown rice   *Serves 4*

This is an ideal supper dish, served on its own with just a large bowl of grated cheese – Parmesan if you have it, or else finely grated Cheddar is nearly as good.

50 g (2 oz) butter
2 tbsp oil
1 green pepper, de-seeded and chopped
1 red pepper, de-seeded and chopped
1 large onion, finely chopped
2 sticks celery, sliced

225 g (8 oz) brown rice
600 ml (1 pint) chicken stock
Salt and pepper
100 g (4 oz) button mushrooms, sliced
75 g (3 oz) cashew nuts
Chopped chives to garnish

Heat the butter in a large pan with the oil, then add the peppers, onion and celery, cover and cook over a moderate heat for 5 minutes. Stir the rice into the pan and cook gently until the butter and oil are absorbed. Blend in the stock, season well and bring to the boil, then reduce the heat, cover the pan and simmer gently for 40 minutes.

Stir in the mushrooms and cook for a further 10 minutes or until the rice is tender and all the stock has been absorbed. Taste and check seasoning and then gently stir in the cashew nuts.

Pile into a warm serving dish and sprinkle the top with chopped chives.

Spaghetti napolitane   *Serves 4*

Put a bay leaf in the water when cooking spaghetti to add flavour.

1 large onion, chopped
1 clove garlic, crushed
2 tbsp oil
794 g (1 lb 12 oz) can peeled tomatoes
2 tbsp tomato purée
1 bay leaf
1 stock cube

$\frac{1}{4}$ level tsp dried mixed herbs or basil
Salt and pepper
1 rounded tsp sugar
350 g (12 oz) long spaghetti
Butter
Plenty of grated Parmesan cheese

Put the onion and garlic in a saucepan with the oil and fry gently for 10 minutes, add the tomatoes, purée, bay leaf, stock cube, herbs, seasoning and sugar and simmer gently for 30 minutes, stirring occasionally so that the tomatoes break up during the cooking.

Meanwhile cook the spaghetti as directed on the packet in fast-boiling water (adding a bay leaf if liked) until just tender, then drain well and reheat in the pan with a large knob of butter; toss until well coated.

Serve the spaghetti in a warm dish and serve the sauce separately. Put a bowl of cheese on the table for everybody to help themselves.

This sauce freezes well; when required thaw at room temperature, then turn into a saucepan and reheat slowly and boil for 1 or 2 minutes.

PIES, PASTIES AND QUICHES

The pie is one of the glories of English traditional cookery. Game pie, steak and kidney pie, fish pie, chicken pie – for family meals and festive occasions they never lose their popularity. Then there are the lighter quiches and flans with their savoury fillings of cheese, bacon and onion. Most pies are best eaten hot or warm; they can be the centrepiece of a formal party, and some can go happily on picnics with crusty bread.

They are easily made too. There is no shame nowadays in using bought frozen pastry, which cuts down on preparation time and is guaranteed to be successful. Or, if you like, you can prepare a batch of your favourite pastry and store it in the freezer until needed.

The finished pies and quiches themselves freeze excellently. Have a pie-making day and store what you do not eat at once. All you have to do then is put the pie in the oven when you want it.

Rabbit charter pie   *Serves 4*

If you can get boneless rabbit for this pie it does save time; otherwise, the meat can be quite easily taken off the bone after stewing, letting the meat get cold enough to handle and then adding it to the thickened sauce. You will need to put a pie funnel or something to support the pastry in the middle of the dish. I find a handle-less cup most useful as I have never had a pie funnel!

62 g (2½ oz) butter
450 g (1 lb) boneless rabbit meat
225 g (8 oz) onions, chopped
350 g (12 oz) carrots, diced

50 g (2 oz) flour
600 ml (1 pt) milk
Salt and pepper
2 thin strips of lemon peel

Suet crust
175 g (6 oz) self-raising flour
75 g (3 oz) shredded suet

1 level tbsp chopped fresh parsley
A little water to mix

Heat the oven to 180° C (350° F), gas mark 4.

Melt the butter in a frying pan and fry the rabbit and onions for 3–4 minutes and then add the carrots and cook for a further minute. Stir in the flour and cook for a minute, then add the milk and bring to the boil, stirring until thickened; season to taste and add the strips of lemon peel.

Turn into a 2 l (3½ pt) ovenproof casserole, cover and cook in the centre of the oven for 45 minutes.

Place the flour and suet in a bowl with a little salt and stir in the parsley. Mix to a soft but not sticky dough with the water and roll out to the size of the casserole and about 1·25 cm (½ in) thickness.

Take the casserole from the oven and turn the heat up to 200° C (400° F), gas mark 6. Remove the lid from the casserole and lift out the strips of lemon peel. Place the suet crust on top of the rabbit. Return to the oven for a further 30 minutes or until the crust is crisp and golden brown.

Quick fish pie   *Serves 6*

Even though this is quick to make from ingredients that you may have in the freezer it is quite delicious.

212 g (7½ oz) packet frozen cod fillets or steaks

212 g (7½ oz) packet smoked haddock fillets

283 g (10 oz) can condensed mushroom soup

397 g (14 oz) packet frozen puff pastry, thawed

1 tbsp chopped parsley

Milk

A sprig of parsley to garnish

Heat the oven to 220° C (425° F), gas mark 7.

Cook the fish as directed on the packets and then flake and remove any skin and bones, put in a bowl and stir in the soup, mix well.

Cut the pastry into 2 pieces, one slightly bigger than the other. Roll out the larger piece into a circle and use to line a shallow ovenproof dish. Spoon in the fish mixture and sprinkle with the parsley and spread flat. Moisten the edge of the pastry with a little cold water. Roll out the remaining pastry to a circle to fit the top of the pie, press edges firmly together and decorate with a fork or knife. Roll out the trimmings, cut into leaves and use to decorate the pie.

Brush the top with a little milk and make two slits in the centre. Bake in the oven for 25–30 minutes until well risen and golden brown. Garnish with a sprig of parsley.

Steak and kidney pie   *Serves 6 (See cover photograph)*

Hardly a week goes by in the winter that we don't have steak and kidney in our house – it is so popular.

450 g (1 lb) stewing steak

225 g (8 oz) ox kidney

25 g (1 oz) flour

25 g (1 oz) dripping

1 large onion, chopped

100 g (4 oz) streaky bacon, cut in strips

300 ml (10 fl oz) beef stock

1 tsp salt

Ground black pepper

100 g (4 oz) mushrooms, sliced

227 g (8 oz) packet puff pastry, thawed

Cut the steak and kidney into 2·5 cm (1 in) pieces and put in a polythene bag with the flour and toss well until coated.

Melt the dripping in a pan, add the meat and fry with the onion and bacon until browned. Stir in the stock and bring to the boil, stirring, add the seasoning and partially cover the pan and simmer for 1½–2 hours or until the meat is tender.

Add the mushrooms and cook for a further 15 minutes, taste and check seasoning and turn into a pie dish and allow to become quite cold.

Roll out the pastry on a lightly floured table and cover the pie, seal and crimp the edges and use any pastry trimmings to decorate the top of the pie. Brush with milk and bake in a hot oven, 220° C (425° F), gas mark 7, for about 30–35 minutes until the pastry is well risen, golden brown and the meat hot through. If by any chance the pastry appears to be getting too brown, cover with a piece of foil.

This pie may be frozen after it has been covered with pastry; cover, label and freeze. To serve: remove the foil, brush the pastry with milk and then bake in the oven as above for 30 minutes, then reduce the temperature to 180° C (350° F), gas mark 4 and bake for a further 20–25 minutes or until the pastry is golden brown and well risen and the meat is hot through.

Game pie   *Serves 6–8*

When you are not too sure of the age of the birds this is an ideal way to make a successful and tender dish.

2 tbsp oil	1 bay leaf
1 stewing pheasant	300 ml (10 fl oz) water
2 pigeons	Salt and pepper
1 large onion, sliced	50 g (2 oz) butter
1 large carrot, sliced	50 g (2 oz) flour
2 sticks celery, sliced	2 tbsp redcurrant jelly
½ bottle red wine	397 g (14 oz) packet puff pastry, thawed

Heat the oil in a large saucepan and fry the pheasant and pigeons until golden brown all over. Drain off any excess oil and add the vegetables, wine, bay leaf and water with plenty of seasoning. Cover the pan and simmer for 1½–3 hours, depending on the age of the birds. Lift out the birds, carve into slices and lay in the pie dish.

Strain the gravy into a small saucepan and discard the bay leaf and add the vegetables to the pie.

Cream the butter with the flour until smooth and add in small pieces to the gravy, whisking until smooth. When all the butter has been added, bring to the boil and simmer until thickened, add the redcurrant jelly and taste the sauce and check seasoning. Pour over the meat and leave to become quite cold. Heat the oven to 220° C (425° F), gas mark 7.

Roll out the pastry and cover the pie, decorate the top with any pastry trimmings, brush and top with a little milk and bake in the oven for 30–35 minutes until the pastry is golden brown and the pie hot through.

This pie may be frozen and should be treated as for steak and kidney pie in the previous recipe.

Sausagemeat puff   *Serves 6*

A firm favourite in our family, quick and easy to make and a recipe which jazzes up basic sausagemeat and makes it sufficient to serve 6.

450 g (1 lb) pork sausagemeat
A little freshly ground black pepper
Salt
1 level tbsp freshly chopped parsley
1 level tbsp freshly chopped mixed herbs

1 small onion, very finely chopped or grated
397 g (14 oz) packet puff pastry, thawed
A little beaten egg to glaze

Heat the oven to 220° C (425° F), gas mark 7.

Put the sausagemeat in a bowl with pepper and a little salt. Add the herbs and onion and mix very thoroughly, then with lightly floured hands shape into a roll 32·5 cm (13 in) long.

Roll out the pastry on a lightly floured table to an oblong 35 × 27·5 cm (14 × 11 in), lay the sausagemeat down the centre of the pastry and make 6 diagonal cuts through the pastry about 5 cm (2 in) apart to within 2·5 cm (1 in) of the sausagemeat.

Brush the edges of the pastry with beaten egg, then alternately wrap the pastry strips over the sausagemeat to form a plait.

Brush all over with beaten egg and bake for 35–40 minutes until the pastry is golden brown. Lift onto a warm serving dish and serve with a gravy or home-made tomato sauce.

Watercress and cheese quiche   *Serves 4–6*

Watercress gives a bright green colour and excellent flavour; chop finely and include some of the stalk.

Pastry
175 g (6 oz) plain flour
100 g (4 oz) butter
40 g (1½ oz) Parmesan cheese, finely grated

About 1 tbsp cold water to mix
1 egg yolk

Filling
2 eggs, beaten
300 ml (10 fl oz) single cream
Salt and pepper
75 g (3 oz) full-flavoured Cheddar cheese, finely grated

1 bunch watercress, finely chopped
25 g (1 oz) butter
1 small onion, finely chopped

Sift the flour into a bowl, add the butter cut in small pieces and rub in with the finger tips until the mixture resembles fine breadcrumbs, stir in the Parmesan cheese. Blend the water with the egg yolks and add to the flour and mix to a firm dough. Roll out on a lightly floured table fairly thinly

and line 22·5 cm (9 in) metal flan tin. Chill in the refrigerator for
15 minutes.

Heat the oven to 220° C (425° F), gas mark 7 with a baking sheet in it.

Line the flan with a piece of greaseproof paper and weigh down with
baking beans and then bake blind for 15 minutes.

Blend the eggs, cream, seasoning, cheese and watercress together in a
bowl. Melt the butter in a small pan and gently cook the onion for about
10 minutes, or until soft but not brown, cool and stir into the filling.

Remove the paper and beans from the flan and pour in the filling, return
to the oven and reduce the heat to 180° C (350° F), gas mark 4 and bake for
25–35 minutes or until the filling is set.

Picnic pie   *Serves 8*

This always looks good and is ideal to take on a picnic for a crowd of
people.

Pastry
275 g (10 oz) plain flour   62 g (2½ oz) lard
62 g (2½ oz) margarine   About 3½ tbsp cold water to mix

Filling
350 g (12 oz) cooked chicken, chopped   3 hard-boiled eggs
225 g (8 oz) cooked ham, chopped   Salt and pepper
225 g (8 oz) pork sausagemeat   A little beaten egg or milk to glaze
1 rounded tsp chopped fresh herbs   298 g (10½ oz) can condensed consommé

Heat the oven to 200° C (400° F), gas mark 6.

Put the flour in a bowl and add the fats cut in small pieces and rub in
with the fingertips until the mixture resembles fine breadcrumbs, add cold
water and mix to a firm dough. Roll out three-quarters of the pastry and
use to line a large loaf tin 22·5 × 12·5 × 7·5 cm (9 × 5 × 3 in).

Place the chicken, ham, sausagemeat, herbs and plenty of seasoning in a
bowl and mix well. Spread half of the mixture over the base of the pie and
make three hollows and place an egg in each, cover with the rest of the
filling and smooth the top.

Roll out the remaining pastry to make a lid, damp the edges of the pie
and press firmly in place, sealing well. Make two slits in the centre of the
pastry and brush the top with a little beaten egg or milk to glaze.

Bake in the oven for 1–1¼ hours until the pastry has shrunk from the
edge of the tin and is golden brown. Remove from the oven.

Gently heat the consommé until just melted and carefully pour into the
pie through the slits. If the pie will not take all the consommé at first you
will find that the rest may be added as the pie cools and absorbs it. When
quite cold, leave the pie overnight in the refrigerator.

Serve cut in slices with salads.

Quiche Lorraine   *Serves 4–6*

Best served warm with a tossed green salad.

Pastry
175 g (6 oz) plain flour   *40 g (1½ oz) lard*
40 g (1½ oz) margarine   *About 6 tsp cold water*

Filling
100 g (4 oz) Gruyère cheese,   *2 large eggs*
* sliced*   *1 tsp chopped fresh parsley*
4 rashers streaky bacon   *1 tsp chopped chives*
150 ml (5 fl oz) single cream *Salt and pepper*

Sift the flour into the bowl and add the fats cut in small pieces and rub in
with the fingertips until the mixture resembles fine breadcrumbs. Add just
sufficient cold water to mix to a firm dough. Roll out the pastry fairly
thinly and use to line a 22·5 cm (9 in) metal flan dish. Chill in the
refrigerator for 15 minutes.

Heat the oven to 220° C (425° F), gas mark 7 and place a baking sheet in
it. Line the flan with a piece of greaseproof paper and weigh down with
baking beans and bake blind for 15 minutes, then remove the paper and
baking beans.

Arrange the cheese slices in the bottom of the flan case. Remove the rind
from the bacon and fry lightly for 1–2 minutes, cut each rasher in half and
arrange spoke fashion on top of the cheese. Mix together the cream, eggs
and herbs with plenty of seasoning. Pour into the flan case and return to
the oven and reduce the heat to 180° C (350° F), gas mark 4 and bake for
25–35 minutes or until the filling is set.

Russian fish pie   *Serves 4*

A tasty pie that is a little different from the usual creamed fish with a
potato topping. Ring the changes by using smoked haddock and prawns or
mushrooms instead of hard-boiled eggs.

350 g (12 oz) cod fillet   *2 tsp lemon juice*
25 g (1 oz) butter   *2 hard-boiled eggs, chopped*
25 g (1 oz) flour   *397 g (14 oz) packet puff pastry,*
300 ml (10 fl oz) milk   * thawed*
1 tbsp chopped parsley   *Beaten egg or milk to glaze*
Salt and pepper

Cook the fish by frying, grilling or poaching; leave to cool, then remove all
the dark skin and bones and flake.

Melt the butter in a pan and stir in the flour and cook for 2 minutes, add
the milk and bring to the boil, stirring until thickened. Add the parsley,

seasoning and lemon juice and mix well. Remove the sauce from the heat and then stir in the eggs and flaked fish. Leave to become quite cold.

Roll out the pastry on a floured table to a 32·5 cm (13 in) square and trim the edges. Place the fillings in the centre and brush the edges with beaten egg or milk, then bring the four corners of the pastry to the centre to form an envelope and seal all the edges firmly. Place on a baking tray and brush with beaten egg or milk and when required bake in a hot oven, 220° C (425° F), gas mark 7, until well risen and golden brown – this will take about 25 minutes. Serve with a green vegetable such as peas or beans.

Great ash pie   *Serves 6*

This is a sort of large Cornish pasty that we used to have on a farmhouse holiday when the children were small. Mrs Slade used to cut the meat up very small by hand and add lots of pepper; she made it in a large Swiss roll tin so that you ended up with lots of filling and not too much pastry. It is best served hot and if liked make a little gravy to go with it. This mixture may also be made into pasties.

Filling
450 g (1 lb) raw minced beef
175 g (6 oz) potatoes, finely diced
100 g (4 oz) carrots, finely diced (optional)

1 large onion, finely chopped
1½ level tsp salt
Plenty of ground black pepper

Pastry
350 g (12 oz) plain flour
75 g (3 oz) margarine
75 g (3 oz) lard

About 4 tbsp cold water
Milk or beaten egg to glaze

Place beef, potato, carrot, onion, salt and pepper in a bowl and mix thoroughly.

Put the flour into a bowl and rub in the fats until the mixture resembles fine breadcrumbs. Add sufficient water to mix to a firm dough. Turn onto a floured table and roll out two-thirds of the pastry into an oblong and use to line a deep Swiss roll tin approximately 27·5 × 17·5 × 3·75 cm (11 × 7 × 1½ in). Put the meat mixture on the pastry and press down evenly. Roll out the rest of the pastry evenly to form a lid. Damp the edges of the pie and cover with the pastry, press the edges well together. Trim off the surplus and crimp the edges. If liked, decorate the top with pastry trimmings.

Brush the top with milk or egg and bake in an oven at 220° C (425° F), gas mark 7 for 20–25 minutes until lightly browned, then reduce the temperature to 180° C (350° F), gas mark 4, and continue to cook for a further 35–40 minutes or until pastry is browned and has shrunk slightly from the sides of the tin.

A remarkably fine fish pie   *Serves 4*

A recipe taken from Mrs Eliza Rundle's book, *A new system of Domestic Cookery*; like many eighteenth-century recipes, anchovies are included in the stuffing. In this version I have used anchovy essence and then served the dish with an anchovy sauce with plenty of parsley added.

4 quarter cut fillets of plaice
1 small onion, chopped
25 g (1 oz) butter
2 tsp anchovy essence
Grated rind of half a lemon

1 rounded tsp chopped parsley
50 g (2 oz) fresh white breadcrumbs
227 g (8 oz) packet puff pastry, thawed
A little egg or milk to glaze

Skin the plaice fillets and place flesh side down on a board.

Put the onion in a pan with the butter and cook gently for 5 minutes, then remove from the heat and add the anchovy essence, lemon rind, parsley and white breadcrumbs and mix thoroughly. Taste and if necessary add a little seasoning. Cool the stuffing then divide into 4 and put a portion on each fillet and roll up.

Roll out the pastry to an oblong 25 × 32·5 cm (10 × 13 in), then put the fillets side by side on the pastry, brush the edges with beaten egg or milk and fold over the pastry to seal. Brush the top with egg or milk and then when required bake in a hot oven, 220° C (425° F), gas mark 7, for about 25 minutes or until the pastry is well risen and golden brown.

Serve with a white sauce which has had a little anchovy essence added to it and some freshly chopped parsley.

Shepherd's pie   *Serves 6*

Traditionally shepherd's pie is made with cooked lamb and cottage pie with cooked beef. In our house the roast joint is so popular that I never have sufficient left for a pie, so I use minced beef and start from scratch.

1 large onion, chopped
2 good-sized carrots, diced
675 g (1½ lb) minced beef
25 g (1 oz) flour
300 ml (10 fl oz) beef stock

2 tbsp tomato purée
Salt and pepper
675 g (1½ lb) cooked mashed potato
Butter

Put the onion, carrots and beef in a large saucepan and cook gently for about 5 minutes to let the fat run out. Stir in the flour and cook for a minute. Blend the beef stock and tomato purée into the pan and then season well, cover and simmer for 45 minutes or until the beef is tender. Turn into an ovenproof dish and cover with the mashed potato, dot with small knobs of butter and cook in a hot oven at 220° C (425° F), gas mark 7 for 20–25 minutes until the top is a pale golden brown.

This freezes well. When making put into a foil container, then cover, label and freeze. To serve: leave to thaw fully at room temperature and then reheat as above but increase the cooking time to about 45 minutes to allow the pie to get hot through.

Spanish tuna pie   *Serves 4 (See colour plate facing page 49)*

A very tasty mid-week pie.

Filling
25 g (1 oz) butter	198 g (7 oz) can tuna fish, drained
25 g (1 oz) flour	2 hard-boiled eggs
300 ml (10 fl oz) milk	Grated rind of half a lemon
Salt and pepper	8 Spanish stuffed green olives, sliced

Pastry
225 g (8 oz) flour	50 g (2 oz) lard
50 g (2 oz) hard margarine	About 2 tbsp cold water

First prepare the filling: melt the butter in a small saucepan and stir in the flour and cook for a minute. Gradually stir in the milk and bring to the boil, stirring until thickened and simmer for two minutes, season to taste. Flake the tuna and chop the eggs and add to the sauce with the lemon rind and olives, mix well and then taste and check seasoning. Cool. Heat the oven to 200° C (400° F), gas mark 6.

Put the flour for the pastry in a bowl and add the fats cut in small pieces and rub in with the fingertips until the mixture resembles fine breadcrumbs. Add sufficient water to mix to a firm dough. Roll out half the pastry and line a deep 20 cm (8 in) enamel plate. Place the filling on top.

Roll out the remaining pastry, damp edges and place on top of the filling. Seal and trim the edges and flute to decorate. Make a hole in the centre for the steam to escape and use any pastry trimmings to make leaves and decorate the top of the pie. Brush with a little milk and bake in the oven for about 25 minutes until golden brown.

SUPPER DISHES

Is it to be instant cooking, like bacon and eggs? Will you have to prepare it in advance, or will it be a mixture of both? It is a fact known to cooks that what appear to the most successful impromptu meals are often the ones that have been given a little thought beforehand.

Supper dishes are lighter and more informal than dinner ones. Even the most festive are easy to digest; they should be colourful, fun to eat, quick to prepare and simple to serve.

The wise cook, faced with the possibility of last minute demands for late meals, keeps a supply of ready-made dishes in the freezer if she has one, has plenty of eggs and cheese on hand and has a quick way with leftovers – the minced remains of the joint perhaps, the odd piece of boiled bacon.

Pancakes are a great standby; they lend themselves to all sorts of savoury fillings, can be made in advance and frozen or cooked on the spot and eaten straight from the pan. Or they can be baked in the oven like a cake, served with a sauce, sprinkled with cheese.

Supper vegetables are best kept simple – new potatoes, plain boiled rice, runner beans, salads.

For guests try one of the varieties of moussaka; for children you can't beat toad in the hole.

Beef croquettes   *Serves 4*

This is an excellent way of using up leftover beef from the joint and makes an ideal supper dish.

1 large onion	350 g (12 oz) cooked minced beef
2 carrots	Salt and pepper
50 g (2 oz) dripping	Beaten egg
50 g (2 oz) flour	Brown breadcrumbs
300 ml (10 fl oz) beef gravy or stock	

Mince the onion and carrots. Melt the dripping in a pan and add the onion and carrot, cover and cook gently for about 10 minutes until soft. Stir in the flour and cook for 1 minute, then blend in the gravy or stock and bring to the boil, stirring until thickened and cook for 2 minutes.

Remove from the heat and stir in the beef and season well; turn onto a plate and leave until quite cold.

Divide the mixture into 12 equal portions and with lightly-floured hands shape into 12 croquettes, then coat in beaten egg and breadcrumbs and chill thoroughly.

Deep fat fry for about 5 minutes over a moderate heat until golden brown and hot through.

To freeze: these freeze very well and may be prepared as far as the coating with egg and crumbs, then freeze in suitable portions. To serve: leave to thaw at room temperature for 2 hours then fry as above.

Sweetbreads à la crème   *Serves 6*

Calf's sweetbreads are the most expensive and have a delicate flavour. Fresh ones are difficult to come by, but good butchers can usually get them. Some freezer centres and butchers have frozen ones. Thaw thoroughly before cooking; this is best done overnight in the refrigerator.

675 g (1½ lb) calf's sweetbreads
A sprig of fresh lemon thyme
300 ml (10 fl oz) chicken stock
150 ml (5 fl oz) dry cider
Salt
Ground black pepper

175 g (6 oz) very small button
  mushrooms
62·5 g (2½ oz) butter
50 g (2 oz) flour
150 ml (5 fl oz) single cream
Plenty of freshly chopped parsley

Soak the sweetbreads in cold water for 2 hours to remove all the blood, drain well, then transfer the sweetbreads to a saucepan and cover with fresh cold water and add a teaspoon of salt. Bring to the boil, very slowly, taking about 5 minutes, then drain off the water again. Pull off any membranes without tearing the sweatbreads.

Rinse out the saucepan and return the sweetbreads to it with the lemon thyme, stock, cider and salt and freshly ground black pepper, bring to the boil, cover and simmer for 10 minutes, then add the mushrooms and cook for a further 5 minutes.

Strain off the stock into a measuring jug, remove the thyme and then put the sweetbreads and mushrooms on one side. Melt the butter in a pan, add the flour and cook for a minute. Blend in the stock and bring to the boil, stirring until thickened. Return the sweetbreads and mushrooms to the pan and reheat until hot through, taste and check seasoning. Just before serving blend in the cream and turn into a hot dish, scatter with parsley and serve with boiled rice and buttered leaf spinach.

Meat loaf with onion gravy   *Serves 8*

A very quick and easy loaf to make; serve hot with onion gravy or, if there is any left over, serve cold sliced thinly with a variety of salads.

Meat loaf
450 g (1 lb) minced beef
450 g (1 lb) pork sausagemeat
100 g (4 oz) fresh white breadcrumbs

2 eggs
2 rounded tbsp chopped parsley
Salt and pepper

Onion gravy
25 g (1 oz) dripping
225 g (8 oz) onions, finely sliced
25 g (1 oz) flour
450 ml (15 fl oz) beef stock

1 tbsp Worcestershire sauce
1 tbsp tomato ketchup
A little gravy browning (if necessary)
Salt and pepper

Heat the oven to 160° C (325° F), gas mark 3.

Place all the ingredients for the meat loaf in a bowl and mix very thoroughly and then turn into a large loaf tin 11·25 × 22·5 cm (4½ × 9 in) and bake in the oven for 1½–2 hours or until when a skewer is put in the centre the juices run out clear. Drain off any excess fat and turn onto a warm dish.

Meanwhile prepare the onion gravy. Melt the dripping in a pan and fry the onions for 10 minutes, stirring occasionally until they are golden brown, then add the flour and cook for about 2 minutes until a pale golden brown. Blend in the stock, Worcestershire sauce, ketchup and bring to the boil, stirring until thickened. Add a little gravy browning if necessary and season to taste. Serve very hot with the meat loaf.

Danish frikadeller with spiced red cabbage   *Serves 4*

These meat balls are something that I always have when lunching at the Danish House. They freeze well too.

225 g (8 oz) boneless pork, minced
225 g (8 oz) pie veal, minced
1 onion, grated
50 g (2 oz) fresh white breadcrumbs
4 tbsp milk

1 egg, beaten
1 tsp salt
A good knob of butter
1 tbsp oil

Mix together the meats, onion, breadcrumbs, milk and egg with the salt and chill in the refrigerator for 1 hour.

Divide the mixture into 12 equal portions and shape into ovals with lightly floured hands and then flatten.

Melt the butter in a large frying pan and add the oil. Fry the Frikadeller over a moderate heat, turning once, for 15 minutes until golden brown on both sides. Serve on a bed of spiced red cabbage.

Spiced red cabbage
50 g (2 oz) butter
1 large onion, chopped
450 g (1 lb) red cabbage, shredded
1 medium cooking apple, peeled, cored
  and sliced
25 g (1 oz) brown sugar
2 tbsp redcurrant jelly
4 tbsp cider vinegar
1 tsp salt

Melt the butter in a pan, add the onion and fry gently without colouring for 5 minutes. Add the remaining ingredients and mix thoroughly, cover and simmer until tender – about 45 minutes. Taste and check seasoning.

Creamy pancake rolls *Serves 4 (Makes 8)*

An ideal way of using leftover chicken.

Batter
100 g (4 oz) plain flour
1 large egg

2 tbsp salad oil
300 ml (10 fl oz) milk and water mixed

Filling
40 g (1½ oz) butter
1 onion, sliced
19·5 g (¾ oz) flour
300 ml (10 fl oz) milk
½ tsp grated lemon rind

1 tsp salt
Pepper
225 g (8 oz) cooked chicken
3 tbsp single cream
2 tbsp grated cheese

Prepare the batter; put the flour into a bowl, make a well in the centre and add the egg, oil and half of the milk and water mixture. Beat to a thick batter for 2 minutes and then stir in the remaining liquid.

Now prepare the filling; melt the butter in a saucepan, add the onion and cook until a pale golden brown. Remove from the heat and stir in the flour and cook for 1 minute. Blend in the milk, stirring, and bring to the boil, simmer for 2 minutes and then add the lemon rind and seasoning. Remove from the heat and add the chicken and cream. Leave to cool.

Now make the pancakes; heat a little oil in a 20 cm (8 in) frying pan. When it is hot pour off any excess oil and spoon about 2 tbsp of the batter into the pan. Tip and rotate the pan so that the batter spreads out and thinly covers the base of the pan. Cook the pancake for about 1 minute until pale brown underneath, then turn it over with a palette knife and cook for another minute. Turn out of the pan and make more pancakes in the same manner until all the batter has been used up.

Divide the filling between the pancakes placing a spoonful in the centre of each. Fold each pancake in half over the filling, then fold rounded edge down in 2 places to form a triangle. Place folded side down in a shallow ovenproof dish. Complete other pancakes, placing them overlapping in the dish. Sprinkle with the cheese and bake for 20–25 minutes in the oven at 190° C (375° F), gas mark 5.

Chicken liver pancakes   *Serves 4*

Chicken livers are less expensive than meat and make a tasty stuffing.

Filling
25 g (1 oz) butter
1 large onion, chopped
 finely
225 g (8 oz) chicken livers

100 g (4 oz) streaky bacon cut in small
 strips
¼ level tsp dried thyme
Salt and pepper

8 pancakes (see creamy pancake rolls in the previous recipe)

Cheese sauce
25 g (1 oz) butter
25 g (1 oz) flour
300 ml (10 fl oz) milk

1 level tsp made mustard
Salt and pepper
75 g (3 oz) grated cheese

Heat the oven to 190° C (375° F), gas mark 5.

Melt the butter in a frying pan and fry the onion, chicken livers and bacon for about 8–10 minutes over a moderate heat. Lift out the chicken livers with a slotted spoon and cut into small pieces – scissors are very good for doing this – then return to the pan, add the thyme and seasoning and mix well. Divide the mixture between 8 pancakes and roll up.

Now make the sauce; melt the butter in a pan and stir in the flour and cook for 1 minute. Add the milk and bring to the boil, stirring until thickened, add the mustard and seasoning and simmer for 2 minutes. Stir in 50 g (2 oz) of the cheese.

Lay the pancakes in a shallow ovenproof dish in a single layer and pour the sauce over; sprinkle with the last of the cheese.

Bake in the oven for 25 minutes.

Savoury pancake cake   *Serves 4*

An unusual way of serving pancakes; cut in wedges like a cake for serving it has a very attractive appearance.

Filling
2 rashers streaky bacon, chopped
450 g (1 lb) minced beef
1 onion, chopped
1 stick celery, chopped

12·5 g (½ oz) flour
150 ml (5 fl oz) stock
2 level tbsp tomato purée
1 level tsp salt
Black pepper

8 pancakes (see creamy pancake rolls previously)

Sauce
25 g (1 oz) butter
25 g (1 oz) flour
300 ml (10 fl oz) milk

½ level tsp made mustard
Salt and pepper
100 g (4 oz) grated Cheddar cheese

First prepare the meat filling; put the bacon, beef, onion and celery in a pan and cook gently for 5–10 minutes to allow the fat to run out. Stir in the flour, then add the stock and bring to the boil, stirring. Add the remaining ingredients, cover and simmer for 30–40 minutes or until tender.

Take an ovenproof dish with a lip or one that is slightly deep. Put one pancake on the bottom and then cover with a thin layer of meat sauce, then put another pancake on top and continue to layer the meat sauce and pancakes, ending with a pancake.

Now make the sauce; melt the butter in a small saucepan, stir in the flour and cook for 1 minute. Blend in the milk and bring to the boil, stirring until thickened and simmer for 2 minutes. Add the mustard and seasoning and 75 g (3 oz) cheese. Spoon the sauce over the pancakes and sprinkle with the remaining cheese and bake in the oven at 190° C (375° F), gas mark 5 for 25 minutes or until hot through and golden brown and bubbling.

Gougère   *Serves 6*

Gougère is the same mixture that you would make for éclairs, a nice change from the normal pastry.

Choux paste
100 g (4 oz) butter
300 ml (10 fl oz) water
150 g (5 oz) plain flour
4 eggs

½ tsp salt
Pepper
1 tsp Dijon mustard
75 g (3 oz) Gruyère cheese, diced

Filling
2 onions, sliced
40 g (1½ oz) butter
2 level tsps paprika pepper
12·5 g (½ oz) flour
300 ml (10 fl oz) chicken stock
100 g (4 oz) button mushrooms,
 quartered

1 tsp salt
Pepper
225 g (8 oz) cooked ham, diced
 ham
1 tbsp grated Gruyère cheese

Grease the sides of a 1·7 l (3 pt) shallow ovenproof dish.

Prepare the choux paste; place the butter and water in a shallow pan and bring slowly to the boil, remove from the heat and toss in the flour, quickly, and stir vigorously with a wooden spoon to a thick paste which clings to the spoon. Leave to cool slightly.

Meanwhile prepare the filling; cook the onions in the butter until soft but not coloured – this will take about 10 minutes. Add the paprika pepper and flour and cook gently for 1 minute, stir in the stock and bring to the boil, stirring. Add the mushrooms and seasoning and simmer for 5 minutes, then leave to cool and stir in the ham.

To complete the choux paste, whisk the eggs and gradually beat into the cooled paste 1 spoonful at a time. This may be done with an electric mixer or in a pan with a wooden spoon. When all the egg has been added the mixture will be stiff enough to just hold its shape. Finally beat in the seasoning, mustard and cheese. Spoon around the edge of the dish to form an even border. Spoon the filling into the centre of the dish and sprinkle with cheese.

Bake in a hot oven 200° C (400° F) gas mark 6 for 35–45 minutes or until the choux paste is well risen and golden brown.

Serve hot straight from the oven with a green vegetable, such as beans or broccoli.

Economical moussaka   *Serves 6*

A good way of using the end of the roast lamb joint, this recipe has had potato slices added to eke out the aubergines, which are expensive.

2 tbsp oil
1 large onion, chopped
1 level tsp rosemary
450 g (1 lb) cooked lamb, minced
Salt

Freshly ground black pepper
350 g (12 oz) potatoes, thinly sliced
2 aubergines cut in 0·6 cm (¼ in) slices
*450 g (1 lb) tomatoes, skinned and
    sliced*

Cheese sauce
25 g (1 oz) butter
25 g (1 oz) flour
300 ml (10 fl oz) milk

50 g (2 oz) Cheddar cheese, grated
Nutmeg
Salt and pepper

Yogurt topping
1 egg
25 g (1 oz) flour
¼ level tsp dry mustard

150 ml (5 fl oz) plain yogurt
Salt and pepper
Paprika pepper

Heat the oil in a frying pan, add onion and cook gently for 2–3 minutes. Add the rosemary and lamb and cook for 5 minutes, stirring; season well.

Make the sauce; melt butter in a pan, add the flour and cook for a minute, blend in the milk and bring to boil, stirring until thickened; stir in cheese, nutmeg, and seasoning.

Place half the potato slices in the base of a 20 cm (8 in) deep casserole. Add half of each of the other ingredients (i.e. onion and lamb, aubergines, tomatoes, cheese sauce), in layers, seasoning each layer of vegetables. Repeat, finishing with a layer of potatoes.

Cook in the oven at 190° C (375° F), gas mark 5 for 1 hour. Then prepare the topping by blending the ingredients together, spoon it over the moussaka and cook for a further 20 minutes.

Dolmas *Serves 4–6*

If you can't get vine leaves use cabbage leaves, which are just as good.

1 small onion, chopped
450 g (1 lb) minced beef
½ tsp mixed dried herbs
1 tsp salt
Pepper

150 ml (5 fl oz) beef stock
75 g (3 oz) cooked rice
12 large vine or cabbage leaves
397 g (14 oz) can peeled tomatoes

Place the onion and minced beef in a frying pan and gently fry for 5 minutes to allow any fat to run out, then drain off. Add the herbs, salt, pepper and stock to the pan and bring to the boil, stirring, then stir in the rice and simmer gently until the stock has been absorbed.

Meanwhile cook the vine or cabbage leaves in boiling water for 2 minutes, then drain well and trim away the thickest part of the stalk. Divide the meat mixture into 12 and place a portion in the centre of each leaf and roll up securely to form a parcel, tucking in the ends. Lay in a single layer in an ovenproof dish. Sieve or purée the contents of the can of tomatoes and pour over the dolmas. Season them and bake in a moderate oven, 180° C (350° F), gas mark 4, for 45 minutes.

Special moussaka *Serves 6–8*

I like to blanch the aubergines instead of using the traditional method of frying; this is I think much nicer and not so fatty.

1 small shoulder of lamb (this gives
about 550–675 g (1¼–1½ lb) minced lamb
225 g (8 oz) onions, chopped
2 cloves garlic, crushed
40 g (1½ oz) flour
1½ level tsp salt

Ground black pepper
1 level tsp coriander seeds, crushed
A little fresh thyme or ¼ level tsp dried
* thyme*
397 g (14 oz) can tomatoes
4 aubergines

Sauce
40 g (1½ oz) butter
40 g (1½ oz) flour
450 ml (15 fl oz) milk
1 level tsp made mustard
Grated nutmeg

Salt and pepper
175 g (6 oz) grated Cheddar cheese
1 egg, beaten
Chopped parsley

Heat the oven to 190° C (375° F), gas mark 5. Butter a large ovenproof dish, 1·7 l (3 pt) or larger.

Turn the minced lamb into a large pan; cook over a low heat at first to let the fat run out from the meat and stir to prevent sticking. When the fat has run freely from the meat add the onions and garlic and increase the heat. Fry to brown the meat for about 15 minutes. If there seems to be an excess of fat, spoon off the surplus. Add flour, stir well, then add salt, pepper, coriander, thyme and contents of can of tomatoes. Bring to the boil and simmer for 5 minutes, check seasoning.

Slice the aubergines into 0·6 cm (¼ in) slices and blanch in a pan of boiling water for 1 minute. This softens the skin and prevents the aubergines discolouring. Drain and then dry on kitchen paper.

Make the sauce by slowly melting the butter in a pan, add flour and cook for 2 minutes. Blend in the milk and bring to the boil, stirring until thickened. Add mustard, nutmeg, salt, pepper and cheese. Cook to let the cheese melt then remove from the heat and cool slightly, add the egg and mix well.

Now assemble the moussaka. First put a layer of half the meat mixture in the dish, cover with half the aubergines, season and then repeat with the rest of the lamb and aubergines, so that you end up with 4 layers. Pour the cheese sauce over.

Bake uncovered for 45 minutes – 1 hour until the moussaka is golden brown. Sprinkle with chopped parsley and serve with hot French bread.

Toad in the hole   *Serves 4*

A schoolboy favourite!

12·5 g (½ oz) dripping

Batter
100 g (4 oz) flour
1 tsp salt

8 large pork sausages

1 egg, lightly beaten
300 ml (10 fl oz) milk and water mixed

Heat the oven to 220° C (425° F), gas mark 7. Put the dripping in a roasting tin with the sausages evenly spaced and put in the oven and heat through until the dripping has melted and is very hot.

Meanwhile put the flour and salt in a bowl, stir in the egg and gradually add the milk and water and mix to a smooth batter. Pour this over the sausages and then return to the oven and cook for 35–40 minutes until the batter is well risen and golden brown. Serve at once.

Cauliflower au gratin   *Serves 6*

Take care not to overcook the cauliflower; the florets should still be crisp. To make a more substantial dish you could serve this with bacon rolls.

900 g (2 lb) cauliflower
40 g (1½ oz) butter
40 g (1½ oz) flour
450 ml (15 fl oz) milk
75 g (3 oz) Cheddar cheese, grated

Salt and pepper
½ level tsp made mustard
1 level tbsp Parmesan cheese, grated
2 level tbsp dried breadcrumbs

Break the cauliflower into florets and cook in boiling salted water until barely tender. Drain, reserving 4 tbsp cooling liquor.

Make a sauce by melting the butter in a saucepan and stirring in the flour, then cook for 2 minutes. Blend in the milk and bring to the boil, simmer for 2 minutes and then remove from the heat. Add the Cheddar cheese, seasoning and mustard and stir well until the cheese has melted. Stir in the cauliflower and the reserved liquor; mix well.

Divide the mixture between 6 individual ovenproof dishes. Mix together the Parmesan cheese with the breadcrumbs and scatter over the top of each dish.

Reheat under a moderate grill for 5 minutes until golden brown and bubbling.

To freeze: this may be cooked and frozen before browning; it is best frozen in one dish then covered, labelled and frozen. To serve: thaw completely and then reheat in a hot oven, 220° C (425° F), gas mark 7, for 25 minutes or until golden brown and bubbling.

Scotch eggs   *Serves 6*

Add a little chopped sage to the sausagemeat as a variation. Take care to dry the hard-boiled eggs first, then toss in flour and carefully mould the sausagemeat around so that there are no cracks which will split during frying.

25 g (1 oz) flour
Salt and pepper
6 small hard-boiled eggs
450 g (1 lb) pork sausagemeat
½ level tsp fresh chopped thyme

½ level tsp fresh chopped mixed herbs
1 egg, beaten
Dried breadcrumbs
Oil for frying

Put the flour into a plastic bag with plenty of seasoning. Shell the eggs and dry them thoroughly on kitchen paper and then put in the bag with the flour and shake so that they are well coated.

Mix together the sausagemeat and herbs and divide into 6 equal portions. Cover each egg with the sausagemeat making sure that there are no cracks in the coating. Brush with beaten egg and then coat in dried breadcrumbs. Chill in the refrigerator for at least 1 hour before frying.

Heat the oil to 190° C (375° F). If you don't have a thermometer, drop a cube of day-old bread into the oil; it should sink to the bottom and then rise to the surface and brown in about 60 seconds.

Fry the eggs in the oil for about 5 minutes until golden brown and the sausagemeat cooked through. Lift out, drain on kitchen paper and leave to become quite cold, then cut in half and serve with salads.

Stuffed large courgettes   *Serves 4*

So often courgettes get larger than you meant them to in the garden, especially after a little rain and a warm spell; this is an ideal way to use them up.

4 large even-sized courgettes
75 g (3 oz) long grain rice
25 g (1 oz) butter
1 small onion, chopped
100 g (4 oz) button mushrooms, sliced

4 rashers back bacon, chopped
Salt
Freshly ground black pepper
1 rounded tsp chopped parsley
1 egg, beaten

Cheese sauce
25 g (1 oz) butter
25 g (1 oz) flour
300 ml (10 fl oz) milk
1 tsp made mustard

A little grated nutmeg
Salt and pepper
100 g (4 oz) Cheddar cheese, grated

Cut the courgettes in half lengthways and scoop the seeds out of the centre. Cook the rice in boiling salted water for 10–12 minutes or until tender; drain and rinse well. Melt the butter in a pan and fry the onion, mushrooms and bacon for 5 minutes. Stir in the rice, salt, plenty of black pepper and the parsley, then stir in the egg to bind.

Arrange the courgettes in a single layer in a shallow ovenproof dish and spoon in the filling. Heat the oven to 180° C (350° F), gas mark 4.

Now make the sauce; melt the butter in a small pan, add the flour and cook for one minute. Add the milk and bring to the boil, stirring until thickened. Add mustard, nutmeg and seasoning and 50 g (2 oz) Cheddar cheese, pour this sauce around the courgettes and sprinkle the top with the remaining cheese. Bake in the oven for 35–40 minutes or until the courgettes are tender.

Fried sweetbreads   *Serves 4*

This is a delicious way of serving sweetbreads; they may be prepared in advance and then just popped in the frying pan when required.

450 g (1 lb) calf's sweetbreads   *Fresh white breadcrumbs*
A little chicken stock   *50 g (2 oz) butter*
1 egg, beaten   *4 rashers back bacon*

Soak the sweetbreads in cold water for 2 hours to remove all the blood; drain well. Place in a saucepan, cover with fresh cold water and add 1 tsp salt and bring very slowly to the boil, taking at least 5 minutes, then drain off the water again and take off any membranes without tearing the sweetbreads.

Put back into a saucepan with just sufficient chicken stock to cover and simmer for 15–20 minutes or until tender. Drain well and leave to become quite cold

Cut any very large sweetbreads in half and then coat in beaten egg and the fresh white breadcrumbs.

Melt the butter in a frying pan and fry gently for about 5 minutes, turning so that the sweetbreads are evenly browned, lift out and then serve with the bacon which has been grilled whilst frying the sweetbreads.

Egg and mushroom au gratin   *Serves 4*

This is an ideal supper dish, quick to make, and all that is needed to serve with it is chunks of crusty bread.

8 hard-boiled eggs   *450 ml (15 fl oz) milk*
40 g (1½ oz) butter   *1 chicken stock cube*
100 g (4 oz) mushrooms, sliced   *Salt and pepper*
40 g (1½ oz) flour   *50 g (2 oz) grated cheese*

Butter a shallow ovenproof dish, cut the eggs in half and place cut side down in the dish. Melt the butter in a small pan and stir in the mushrooms; cook for 5 minutes over a gentle heat. Add the flour and mix well and cook for 1 minute, then blend in the milk and stock cube and bring to the boil, stirring until the sauce has thickened; simmer for 2 minutes then taste and check the seasoning.

Spoon the sauce over the eggs and sprinkle the top with the cheese. Brown under a moderate grill and then serve at once with chunks of bread.

Index